D0560250

PENN HILLS LIBRARY
1037 STOTLER ROAD
PITTSBURGH, PA 15235

A NOVEL OF THE MARVEL UNIVERSE

IRON MAN

DEC 2016

JAV

EXTREMIS

PENN HILLS LIBRARY

A NOVEL OF THE MARVEL UNIVERSE

IRON MAN EXTREMIS

MARIE JAVINS

ADAPTED FROM THE GRAPHIC NOVEL BY WARREN ELLIS AND ADI GRANOV

IRON MAN: EXTREMIS PROSE NOVEL.
Published by MARVEL WORLDWIDE, INC.,
a subsidiary of MARVEL ENTERTAINMENT, LLC. OFFICE OF PUBLICATION:
135 West 50th Street, New York, NY, 10020.
Copyright © 2014 Marvel Characters, Inc. All rights reserved.

ISBN# 978-0-7851-6519-4

All characters featured in this issue and the distinctive names and likenesses thereof,
and all related indicia are trademarks of Marvel Characters, Inc. No similarity between
any of the names, characters, persons, and/or institutions in this magazine with those of
any living or dead person or institution is intended, and any such similarity which may
exist is purely coincidental.

Printed in the U.S.A.

ALAN FINE, EVP - Office of the President, Marvel Worldwide, Inc. and EVP & CMO
Marvel Characters B.V.; DAN BUCKLEY, Publisher & President - Print, Animation
& Digital Divisions; JOE QUESADA, Chief Creative Officer; TOM BREVOORT, SVP
of Publishing; DAVID BOGART, SVP of Operations & Procurement, Publishing; C.B.
CEBULSKI, SVP of Creator & Content Development; DAVID GABRIEL, SVP of Print
& Digital Publishing Sales; JIM O'KEEFE, VP of Operations & Logistics; DAN CARR,
Executive Director of Publishing Technology; SUSAN CRESPI, Editorial Operations
Manager; ALEX MORALES, Publishing Operations Manager; STAN LEE, Chairman
Emeritus. For information regarding advertising in Marvel Comics or on Marvel.
com, please contact Niza Disla, Director of Marvel Partnerships, at ndisla@marvel.
com. For Marvel subscription inquiries, please call 800-217-9158. **Manufactured
between 11/6/2013 and 12/9/2013 by SHERIDAN BOOKS, INC., CHELSEA, MI,
USA.**

First printing 2014
10 9 8 7 6 5 4 3 2 1

COVER AND INTERIOR ART BY ADI GRANOV

Stuart Moore, Editor

Design by Spring Hoteling

Senior Editor, Special Projects: Jeff Youngquist

SVP of Print & Digital Publishing Sales: David Gabriel

Editor In Chief: Axel Alonso

Chief Creative Officer: Joe Quesada

Publisher: Dan Buckley

Executive Producer: Alan Fine

Three people—Steve Buccellato, David Wohl, and Marc Siry—convinced me to hang around Marvel after my internship in 1988. I stayed thirteen years before leaving. Warren, Bob, and Polly kept me there, then Stuart brought me back as a writer in 2012. This story is for them.

PROLOGUE

Tony Stark, the invincible Iron Man, hadn't been much of an athlete as a kid. But then, he wasn't the last one on the playground picked for kickball, either. He'd been a precocious child genius, heir to the Stark Enterprises fortune—sure, everyone knew that. But at least he hadn't embarrassed himself in gym class. Being a brainiac didn't have to mean being a clichéd egghead. Geek chic had been around a lot longer than today's magazines and tabloids would have us believe.

But the tabloids would have you believe all kinds of stuff. Like that Tony Stark was a superficial dilettante, a wealthy opportunist, and a billionaire playboy.

Maybe the last bit was true. Or had been. Tony was trying to live down the one-night stands. But when women he barely remembered were quoted in 40-point type across the cover of the *World-Star* as suggestively saying "NOTHING IRON ABOUT STARK," it got tough to ignore the headlines, fabricated or otherwise.

The rest—the stuff about him being a wealthy jerk—was completely false. At least, it wasn't the whole story. Tony occasionally behaved poorly, but he'd learned compassion when he'd become Iron Man. Or partial compassion. Was there such a thing as partial compassion? Tony wondered as he scraped his forehead on the sidewalk outside Dubai's convention center. He didn't feel compassionate. He felt ticked off.

He heard a man's voice from the other side of the fountain: "There's no way that rich weasel outran us." Tony was lucky to have a stronger attachment to pragmatism than to dignity, or he'd have been embarrassed to be hiding below the far side of a fountain rim.

"I don't know, Joe, he's pretty fit." That was a woman's voice now. Tony vaguely recognized it—she was a television reporter. Had he seen her naked some years back, maybe after too late a casino night during the Vegas electronics show?

He didn't have time to think about it. "Is that a foot?"

Busted. Tony could leave his shoe, delay them a few more seconds. But he liked these shoes, and he'd already gotten sand on his suit. He crawled a few feet, hoping to make it to the parking structure next door to the convention center.

He hadn't thought the paparazzi would be outside the exit of the Dubai Emergent Technologies Expo, waiting to ambush the famous Tony Stark with their cameras and microphones. He hadn't given the immediate future a lot of thought on that day, just a few weeks ago, when he'd impulsively admitted to the world that he was the super hero the media had christened Iron Man. It hadn't occurred to him he would become the hottest tabloid story since…well, since no one. Tony was sure he was way more famous than Princess Diana or Michael Jackson had ever been.

"Mister Stark."

Tony looked up to see a giant SLR lens pointing at his face.

"You must be Joe." The cameraman's face reddened as he realized Tony had overheard his "rich weasel" remark.

Click. Beep. Click. Beep. Click. Now a half-dozen other cameras were on tripods and pointed at Tony's face, along with three microphones.

Tony jumped to his feet. Reporters pressed in, crushing each other's gear in their zeal to get closer.

"Mister Stark," the cameraman slowly rolled out the syllables. "Whatever were you doing lying on the sidewalk? Don't you know that Dubai gets *hot* this time of year?"

"Of course," said Tony. "Stark Enterprises is working on a new piece of equipment that cools sidewalks. For your information, heat is the number-one cause of…"

He thought rapidly. Sidewalks were more likely to degrade with cold, not heat.

"…sidewalk-buckling. When sidewalks buckle, they become uneven. Someone could fall. A dachshund could trip, you know, with those short little legs. Look, like right there."

Tony pointed to a perfect, level slab of concrete. No one else even glanced.

"Mister Stark." Joe was talking again. "How do you expect Stark Enterprises to make money now that you've abandoned your lucrative weapons contracts with the military?" Joe smirked. "Do you intend to have Iron Man perform in the circus?"

"Joe, are you suggesting I'm wrong to work for world peace?"

"I'm suggesting you've overlooked your responsibilities to your board, stockholders and employees."

Tony couldn't win this argument. He wasn't going to suddenly declare a renewed interest in building weapons.

The other reporters all fired away with their questions, yelling louder and louder as they tried to be heard over each other.

"…Iron Man…weapons…public safety…her name…"

Tony backed slowly up against the fountain as the crowd pressed in. This time, instead of dropping to the sidewalk, he leapt into the fountain, getting good and drenched as he ducked across it and out the other side. He ran to the parking structure, glad for the small delay as his pursuers gathered their tripods and gear. Tony hurried up a set of stairs to the second level. He had just enough of a head start that he was able to throw himself off the side of the structure without the reporters seeing him.

He landed on the sand below. *Oof.* Tony ducked and fled to the other side of the convention center. He tried the doors, but they only opened from inside—this wasn't the main entrance. He spotted a pair of wooden railings next door, lining a walkway that led to a tall, concrete barrier. Tony realized he'd stumbled on to an outdoor arena. *Good.* Let the reporters look for him at the convention center's exit or in the parking structure.

Tony loved attention, sure. But when he'd told the world he was Iron Man and that Stark Enterprises was changing its focus, he'd only been prepared for the fawning--not for the incessant questioning about his past work and vocal doubts about his sincerity. He certainly didn't expect the fictional headlines the tabloids had generated, or the salacious—and utterly false—rumors about his friends and colleagues.

He entered the arena, sat down on the grandstand around the dusty center track, and pulled out his phone.

"Call Pepper."

The screen flickered and darkened. Out of power. Again. He'd have to check the phone team's progress when he got back to the States. The world needed a Stark phone. *He* needed a Stark phone.

Something wet and mushy brushed up against Tony's ear. He jumped and looked up to see a spindly legged camel gazing at him through long lashes. *Yuck.*

Wet camel nose. And what was that on the camel's back? A type of saddle, but the rider wasn't human.

There'd been a mention of this in the Expo program, Tony remembered. The latest in robot camel-jockeys were on display. He'd been speaking on a panel and had missed the demonstration. Sensors placed on the camel's chest, knees, and mouth sent data to the robots and to the camel's trainer. The robots would then artificially evolve, assessing future moves based on each measurement, every experience, and factors such as wind and sand. To the untrained and unscientific eye, the robot jockeys appeared capable of learning, instead of being piloted remotely by trainers as they had been in the past.

Tony laughed as he saw a plastic Robby the Robot bobblehead on top of the robot. Someone had been playing with a 3D printer. The rest of the robot was just a steel box covered in what looked like a giant tube sock.

"Hold still," murmured Tony to the camel as he reached up to the saddle. He wanted that robot. Not just out of curiosity—he was dying to get a look at the internal specs—but also because Tony knew that where there was a robot, there was a power source.

He was going to use this robot jockey to jump-start his phone.

Tony loosened the straps that held the robot in place and slid it out of its sock. He unclasped two small metal hooks that held an access panel, and then opened up the robot to get to the battery.

"Mister Iron Man. May I be of some assistance?"

A middle-aged Afghani man in a white shalwar kameez, vest, and sandals stood in front of Tony.

"Oh, hello. I'm just going to…borrow your camel pilot for a minute." Tony flashed a smile.

"Do as you must, Mister Iron Man. I can put my robot back together."

"Thanks…uh…"

"Call me Ahmed."

"Thanks, Ahmed. Please call me Tony. You like robots? Or camel racing? Or both?"

"Electronics. I have always enjoyed circuits and robots. But where I am from, we have only a few opportunities in electronics."

"Funny, isn't it?" Tony chatted idly while he dismantled the robot with his fingers and a pen cap. He grabbed the battery pack and tugged it from its clip. "Afghanistan has some of the biggest lithium deposits in the world…"

"…but no industry to use it." Ahmed laughed now. "My brother, he always said this, too. He also loved science."

Tony hesitated now, hearing the regret in Ahmed's voice.

"Where is your brother now?" Tony spoke softly as he plugged the battery pack into his phone. The phone lit up, the word "charging" flickering across the screen.

"He joined a militia. There were no science jobs. Or any jobs. A defect in his own gun killed him."

"Was it…was it a Stark weapon?" Tony's phone was flashing tomorrow's headlines across the screen now—

hacking into newspaper previews was a cinch—along with SMS messages, missed calls, and the time on three continents. But Tony could not look away from Ahmed.

"No, Mister Stark. It was a cheap counterfeit from Pakistan. A fake. A Stark gun would never have exploded."

Tony tightened his lips and nodded. His innocence in this matter was only a technicality. Tony had participated in the industry of war, profited from the deaths of others like Ahmed's brother. Ahmed continued to smile, but with the worn look of a man tired of smiling.

Now a headline on Tony's phone caught his eye. "RED HOT PEPPER POTTS! THE SEXY STORY STARK DOESN'T WANT THE WORLD TO KNOW!"

Oh no, he thought. *The World-Star has gone too far. Everything they say about me is partially justified. But Pepper is an innocent.*

Tony e-mailed Stark's legal team with a link to the headline and instructions to threaten the publisher with every possible action if they printed lies about his assistant. Then he called Pepper.

"Tony, where are you? You have meetings with emergent-tech experts at three—and a half-hour ago, too!" She was annoyed but not frantic. She didn't know about the headlines.

"Paparazzi," he explained. "Pepper, can you do two things for me? First, I need an extraction. A security detail to get me past reporters, and then on to the plane home. Have Happy set up living quarters for me somewhere safe—try the Coney Island workshop. Tell him to hang around—I'm going to stay there a while, let things calm down."

"Of course. I've been wondering when you were going to need a vacation from this madness. Why you told everyone you're Iron Man is—"

"Pepper, wait. The second thing. It's important."

She paused.

"I have an urgent classified assignment for you. No one else can be trusted with this. Pack anti-malarial meds, your vaccination certificate, rehydration salts, and business clothes to last at least a month. You leave immediately. All communications will be strictly through encrypted Stark satellites. I'll send you details as soon as I'm on the plane and can plug in. Go."

Suddenly tired, Tony leaned back on the grandstand. His shoes were ruined, and his pockets might never be empty of sand again. Ahmed tinkered with the robot, while the camel sniffed the dirt on Tony's suit. More alerts popped up on Tony's phone, so he shut it off.

He left it off for a long time.

The headlights of Nilsen's gray 1990 Econoline van illuminated the crossroads ahead on the outskirts of Bastrop, Texas.

"Don't run the stop sign, Nilsen," hissed Beck from the passenger seat. "We don't need to get pulled over tonight."

"Tonight?" The larger man braked, and then glared at Beck. "You think I want to get pulled over any night? I got no insurance and a warrant for unpaid parking tickets in San Marcos. I don't need anyone running my license."

"You don't have a license, dumbass," growled Mallen from the darkened back of the van, where he crouched against the sliding door. "Put on your seatbelts. If any unexpected guests show up, we have to split in a hurry. You're ugly enough without glass in your chin."

"There's no security, Mallen. I told ya, my cousin worked there," said Beck. "Ain't no one there now. Abandoned since the fires. Creepy. Not even the rats go in."

"That's cuz they all died, Beck. When the fire burned out the power and the slaughterhouse was blocked off, it's not like the firemen went in to recover the slabs of beef. The rats gnawed their way in, but died from the putrid meat. Dead rats and rancid meat rotting for weeks—not even the illegals go in there. Half of Bastrop reeked for four months 'til the sheriff finally broke in to find the source of the smell."

"You sure this is a good idea, Mallen?" Nilsen looked back, his shaved head visible in the rearview mirror. "You'll be stuck in there a week. All by your lonesome. We can't help you once this starts."

"Three days. They cleaned it up."

"Yeah, so now it just stinks of ammonia."

The Econoline pulled up in front of an unlit building. D. R. Cole Slaughterhouse had specialized in grass-fed beef and pasture-fed pork until the Feds had come in with their truth-in-advertising witch-hunt.

"Whatever. We're not here for the atmosphere.

We're here cuz it's empty and no one is gonna mess with me."

Mallen took a last swig of his Shiner Bock, reached out the window over Beck's shoulder and hurled the brown bottle at the cracked concrete doorframe of the brick slaughterhouse. The glass shattered against stained graffiti and leftover paste from "No Trespassing" signs.

"Bombs away," chuckled Beck.

Mallen unlatched the van's back door and stepped to the street. The sliding door on the side hadn't worked since Nilsen had deliberately sideswiped a Volvo station wagon outside an organic grocery in Austin.

"Bring the briefcase," he said as he walked to the heavy wooden doors of the slaughterhouse and pushed them open. "Be careful."

Beck and Nilsen followed Mallen into the dark, concrete halls of the empty slaughterhouse, Beck handling the briefcase with uncharacteristic gentleness. Mallen led them into a large cold room—its power long ago disabled, floors and walls scrubbed clean of the remnants of steers, hogs, and rats.

As Beck bent to the ground to open the briefcase, Mallen turned back to the door, glancing one last time at the hallway leading to the exit. The Econoline's headlights shone faintly from outside, tempting him back, as if the past were still accessible from just behind the door. But if what Beck had in the briefcase did what it was supposed to do, Mallen wouldn't need the Econoline or his friends or the man he'd been. He'd be stronger, faster, smarter. He'd do what the world needed—help it, in a way. Put it back on track.

He turned away from the door, back toward Beck and Nilsen.

Beck had unlatched the briefcase and pivoted the lid up. The three men stared at the contents: a jet injector and two small, black cartridges held in place by gray molded plastic.

Mallen realized he might end up dead from this injection. He watched as Beck assembled the injector, loaded the gas cartridges in one by one to power the liquid jets.

"Mallen, you sure you're up for this?" Beck hesitated.

"Just do it," snarled Mallen, more fiercely than he'd intended. He knelt on the concrete floor.

Nilsen towered in front of Mallen, placing a steadying hand on either side of Mallen's head. Mallen focused on the big man's beer belly, which poked out under a black T-shirt. Nilsen had tried to cover it up as always, under an oversized olive-green zippered hoodie. But there was no missing the gut at the moment, since it was all Mallen had to look at if he didn't want to stare right into Nilsen's eyes while his life transformed.

Beck fixed the jet injector against the back of Mallen's neck, just between Mallen's brown hair and the tan leather jacket he'd worn steadily for the last decade, even in the summer.

Beck applied pressure to the trigger with his index finger. *Psssht.* The liquid squeezed through the injector's tip, past Mallen's pores, and then on into his bloodstream.

"Aaoooww!" Mallen jumped as the serum mixed with his blood, delivering what felt like a tingling electric shock. The shock grew stronger, until Mallen could barely stand it. His eyes bulged, and he bared his teeth as he lunged away from Beck. Nilsen let go of Mallen's head and jumped clear.

Mallen fell to his knees, spitting with surprise.

"Hnf!" He couldn't speak. Both his hands involuntarily went to the spot on his neck where the serum had entered his bloodstream.

Take it out. Stop it. Hurts. Mallen seized up, clenched, and then slumped over like a dead man.

For a long moment, Mallen couldn't move or hear. Then a buzzing began. Where was the buzzing? His own head, he realized. The noise slowed, became his thudding pulse. Then, from a distance, he heard Nilsen, his voice muffled as if he were in the next room.

"Nothing's happening, Beck. Something should be happening."

Mallen coughed, moved slightly, and cleared his throat. He started to sit up.

"Hgk."

"Listen," said Beck. "I, uh, I guess we were sold a dud. Get your breath back, Mallen. We'll get back in Nilsen's van and, y'know, start again. It's not over yet."

"Hgkk." Mallen swore as he struggled to rise, his hand covering his eyes.

Then Mallen felt the serum in every molecule—in

his head, his limbs, his guts. And it hurt. He was on fire inside, in wrenching pain.

"HHHEEEGGHH!" He howled, his face contorted, veins bulging, eyes full of blood and fear. His guts were melting, he was sure of it, his organs collapsing and liquefying—turning into a thick black liquid, which he violently retched on to the cold-room floor.

Beck bolted. He was halfway to the exit before Nilsen stopped gaping and raced to follow him. Mallen heard the steel door slam shut, the brace slide into place, the sounds of footsteps receding back toward the Econoline. And then he heard nothing else over the escalating thumping in his head.

Mallen was alone, locked in the abandoned slaughterhouse.

He shuddered, gasped, and collapsed. Warm liquids streamed from his nose, mouth, and ears. His mouth felt full and tasted bitter, metallic. Blood, he thought, tastes like dirty pennies.

Lying on the cold concrete of the slaughterhouse, Mallen's violent body contractions and spasms slowly passed. His head still hurt like hell, but he no longer heard his pulse, and his breathing had gone from quick and shallow to barely perceptible. Was this death? How could it not be? He lay silently in a pool of his own steaming, liquefied innards.

Smells like hell, he thought. Should've asked Beck to make sure the rats are really gone.

He convulsed one last time and passed out.

O N E

"MISTER STARK."

Tony rolled over as the deafening, crackling electronic voice boomed through his garage.

"MISTER STARK. WAKEY-WAKEY, RISE AND SHINE."

Tony groaned and sat up on his cot, pushing his blanket aside as he searched for the source of the voice. He spotted it, then halfheartedly tossed a sweat-stained pillow at the wall speaker. It fell short of its target.

"Go easy on the reverb, will you? I'm trying to sleep here."

"Do you know who this is, Mister Stark?"

"No." Tony scowled with irritation.

"This is Mrs. Rennie. I'm your temporary personal secretary. Do you know who you are?"

"Not a clue."

He thought momentarily of ways to take revenge on Pepper for hiring this retired Brooklyn high-school algebra teacher over the former Rockette from the temp agency.

"It's time for you to come out of that disgusting garage and greet the world, Mister Stark."

Tony wrinkled his forehead and considered getting up, but he'd become quite fond of his garage, not to mention his cot. How, he wondered, had Mrs. Rennie patched herself into the surround-sound intercom system? He glanced at his phone on the floor, a few feet away from the cot, nearly lost among a jumble of wires, devices, socks, and chargers. Ten missed calls from Mrs. Rennie this morning alone, all within the last half-hour. *Ah. Desperation, then.*

He responded with eloquence befitting the moment. "Bite me."

"Young men like you used to respect their elders, Mister Stark."

"Two thousand years ago, we used to send our elders into the desert to die when they started bugging us." Tony swung his bare legs off the cot and on to the garage floor. He caught an alarming whiff of himself. How long had he been wearing this black T-shirt and boxers?

"And now we have salaries and Winnebagos. Life is tough." Mrs. Rennie turned down the reverb to talk business. "You have that ridiculous interview set for ten."

Tony groaned and put his forehead into his hands. He thought about potential ways out of this, came up with none, then looked back up.

"Bellingham? Already?"

"You made the appointment weeks ago, Mister Stark. I *did* suggest you avoid it and attend a board meeting instead."

Weeks. He'd been in here for weeks. The garage had no windows, and he'd lost track of the transition from day to night as he'd alternately slept and tinkered. How many carry-out food containers sat over there next to the server array? How much Chinese food had Happy brought him? How many shawarmas? Where was Happy? Wasn't it time for breakfast?

Tony stood up. He wanted to meet Bellingham—a legend among do-gooders and documentary filmmakers—for personal reasons. Time to emerge.

"Okay. What's the time?"

"Eight a.m., Mister Stark." Mrs. Rennie was gloating with triumph now.

"Eight. Eight in the morning." Tony was silent a beat. There was no reason he had to be up this early. "You sadist."

"Terrible things happen to those who don't respect their elders, Mister Stark."

"But *you* started…"

He saw an alert pop up on his laptop, across the room on the steel workbench. Pepper was IMing from Kinshasa. But he was avoiding Pepper. He'd sent her out of the country to research his confidential project, sure, but also because he didn't want her to hear about the crass—and presumably false—allegations made by the gossip columnist at *World-Star* magazine. But maybe it was time—time to get up, shave, catch up on the status of the multinational corporation that bore his name, check on the legal team's progress on stopping *World-Star*, and emerge from his garage-cocoon. At least then he could stop avoiding talking to Pepper. He missed her cheerfulness and her honesty, though he liked it when she became uncharacteristically angry with him, as she was bound to be when she learned he'd been hibernating, hiding from the world.

At least then he'd have her undivided attention.

"Okay, Mrs. Rennie. Have some fresh clothes and coffee sent to the garage. The gallon-drum of coffee. And possibly some kind of intravenous drip." Tony leaned back, stretching his shoulders and listening to his neck crack as he swiveled his head from side to side.

She'd better not make it decaf. That would be just like Mrs. Rennie to pretend she hadn't understood his directive.

The alert on his laptop vanished as he crossed the room and headed to the shower.

Tony shaved and carefully groomed his vandyke— that combination of beard and mustache that the kids had taken to calling a "Tony Stark" ever since the day he'd impulsively admitted to the world that he was Iron Man. He chuckled, then caught a glimpse of himself laughing in the bathroom mirror. He winced, squinted, and turned sideways. He tried to remember what it had been like to see a suave player in the mirror—a brilliant, self-absorbed billionaire that women wanted. But all he saw was the worried face of regret on a man who had ruined thousands of lives with his weapons, a man who didn't deserve to still be alive after so many others had died from his inventions.

A man deserving of scorn.

He looked down quickly, then slowly lifted his head again.

"What're you looking at?" He stared hard at himself, willing the brash and brilliant Tony Stark of old to possess him, at least long enough to get through this interview.

Remember who you were before Afghanistan. Strong. Capable. Free of self-doubt, until your eyes were opened to the tragedy your profiteering had wrought upon others.

You were superficial, he reminded himself.

And so he lost the staring contest with his own reflection. It wouldn't agree to his delusions of grandeur, no matter how temporary. He turned away.

"I hate it when you look at me like that," said Tony over his shoulder.

He emerged an hour later, crossing the courtyard from his garage to the rear service entrance of the main Stark Enterprises Coney Island headquarters.

As Tony entered the reception area off the lobby, Happy looked up, startled, from playing a word game on his phone. Had he been here the whole time Tony had been holed up? Was that why his chauffeur had always been available to pick up his meals? Tony nodded to Happy.

"Nice of you to make an appearance, Mister Stark." Mrs. Rennie pushed her dollar-store reading glasses down her nose and peered at Tony. She had been snarling into her phone, but had hung up when she saw an opportunity to berate Tony, which was much more fun than planning conferences.

Tony started to reply, then spotted a crowd of demonstrators outside the window, past the perimeter fence. When they saw him, they held up signs, but he couldn't quite make out the distant writing.

"What are they doing here? I thought they quit protesting when we got out of the weapons business."

"Protesting? No. They want to see your counterpart, your so-called Iron Man. That irate mob, Mister Stark, they are your..." She shuddered. "...*admirers*."

A broad smile spread over Tony's face. He had fans. *Of course.* Or did Iron Man have fans? He thought for a second, trying to differentiate between fans of Iron Man and fans of Tony Stark. *Ah, same thing.* He *was* Iron Man now, ready to help the world, defend the helpless, and make up for years of weapons profiteering. His earlier moment with the mirror was forgotten now. *Of course they love me. What's not to love?*

But more important, he had an opportunity here. One he couldn't pass up.

"How did they know I was here?"

"Might I suggest that the next time you aim for anonymity and discretion, you do not first pose for dozens of cell-phone photos with the Coney Island Sideshow's acrobatic-mermaid weekend burlesque squad?"

"Mrs. Rennie, even half-fish women deserve to be treated with a bit of respect. How long have my adoring fans been waiting to see me?"

"They are here daily, Mister Stark. They've been here since you holed up in your filthy man cave. I don't know where they sleep, or even if they sleep."

"Well, get them port-a-potties! Get them water and snacks! Don't just leave them standing there waiting to see me."

"Oh, I didn't." She smiled. "I had Happy walk around the lobby in an Iron Man Halloween costume." Happy suddenly became very absorbed in his word game.

"Nice work. But there's something else I want to do for them."

He waited a moment, so his next directive would have maximum effect. He smiled sweetly at Mrs. Rennie, and she tensed up.

"Here's two hundred bucks." Tony pulled two crisp bills from his wallet. "Be a peach and take them all on the Wonder Wheel, would you? Tell them it's courtesy of their brilliant pal, Tony Stark. Nono, make that Iron Man."

Mrs. Rennie glared at Tony and did not reach her hand out. He dropped the money on to her keyboard and smiled as big a smile as he could muster.

"Buy them some funnel cake, too, my dear. Or corn on the cob if they don't do gluten. Is there gluten in funnel cake? Happy, can you look that up? No, call Pepper. Ask her if there's gluten in funnel cake. And if it's called funnel cake in Coney Island, or if Mrs. Rennie should order it by saying *zeppole*. Use the Stark satellite line—Pepper's in Kinshasa this morning. Be sure to ask her if they have funnel cake in Kinshasa, too. We've got to make sure she's taking care of herself by snacking once in a while." He turned back to Mrs. Rennie. "Thanks so much. You're fab. I hope Pepper never comes home so that we can continue to have these warm and tender moments together."

Over in the corner, Happy snorted coffee out of his nose. Mrs. Rennie glared at him icily. "Mister Hogan," she said. "For those who cannot consume gluten or corn, you are tasked with winning them stuffed bears at the archery shoot. If there are no stuffed bears, I will supply you with the necessary materials to *sew them yourself.*"

Tony waved enthusiastically through the window to his fans, who pushed and jostled each other to get a better view of their hero.

Tony snapped his fingers and pointed with both hands at the crowd, smiling broadly. He winked at Happy, who was trying hard to recover his composure.

Tony whirled around and strode purposefully through the sliding elevator doors. As they closed behind him, he laughed and relaxed—*the look on Mrs. Rennie's face!*—then remembered the surveillance camera on the elevator ceiling. He mouthed the words "Good morning, Mrs. Rennie" at the camera, then slowly, deliberately scratched his chin with his middle finger.

......

Meanwhile, in Austin, Texas, Dr. Aldrich Killian sat at his brown desk in a drab room. Why, he wondered, had Futurepharm opted for such a bland office, out here in this boxy two-level pre-fab building in a generic office park? They were dependent on erratic contracts, certainly, and that in itself had exiled them north of Parmer Lane, halfway to Pflugerville, to a discounted non-neighborhood far from shops and restaurants. But surely paint didn't cost more if it had a bit of color in it. Dr. Killian spent most of his waking hours in this beige box, working feverishly against the clock to come in under impossibly tight budgets while scoring moderately successful medical breakthroughs. He'd had to make sacrifices enough in his personal life. Would it have killed Futurepharm to add a bit of cozy pleasantness to the spot in which he seemed to spend his entire life?

"Yes, the special-projects vault has been compromised." Dr. Killian heard his colleague, Dr. Maya Hansen, speaking to a *Statesman* reporter on the phone in the next boxy office. "Yes, we're working on that now, as I told your colleague at the *Chronicle*. Yes, I understand you are from a different newspaper, but I still have to refer you to General Fisher as we have protocols to maintain. No, no, Dr. Killian is coordinating efforts from this end."

Maya was snapping at the journalist, speaking sharply while anxiously trying to get off the phone. She had even less patience with the media than Dr. Killian did. Like him, she put in long hours here at Futurepharm. And the whole team was short-tempered at the moment, after the events of the last few days.

"They know Extremis has been extracted from the vault." Dr. Killian went back to a Word document he'd begun typing last night. "It's chaos outside my blessed door. This place is so badly organized; no one seems to know what has been stolen or what to do about it."

He paused now, wrinkled his brow, tapped a finger on his desk, and contemplated his next words. He wished he had a cigarette. Long before Maya Hansen had joined Futurepharm, when she was still a college student dazzling biology professors and thinking about a career in science, Dr. Killian had quit smoking under pressure from the board during the AeroVapor emphysema research trials. He'd used electronic cigarettes for months to wean himself off tobacco. At least with those, he hadn't had to go stand outside in the sun every time he wanted a smoke. He wished he had one now to calm his nerves and help shut out the angry sound of Maya barking at the journalist, even though he knew logically that it wouldn't have worked.

Maya was a young and attractive woman, but also brilliant and opinionated. Dr. Killian wasn't as smart, even with decades more experience and wisdom, and that bothered him. But Maya had few peers. *Just as well*, he thought. *She's got no time for peers, friends, or relationships. Maybe no patience for us lesser humans, even. It's got to be tough to be that brilliant.* Her contributions had rocketed Extremis ahead by a decade. They'd be nowhere near it working, certainly not approaching its release, if she hadn't been head researcher on the project team. Without Dr. Hansen's innovative approach and unique research, Extremis would be little more than a concept that Killian tinkered with on weekends.

"Maya Hansen was in here earlier," typed Dr. Killian, "She was shouting at me. She always shouts, never happy.

"It's only a matter of time before the thief is discovered and interrogated. I know I won't make it through an interrogation. I can barely get through sitting at lunch in the cafeteria without blurting out the truth to the person next to me. Or to the dishwasher. The cashier. To anyone. I know that I loosed something terrible."

Dr. Killian could see his reflection in his computer monitor. He looked tired, old, worn out. He still had all his hair, and it wasn't gray all over yet—it was beige, like everything else in the room. But his years of practically living in the lab—from grant to grant, project to project—had left his face lined and exhausted.

"Knowing that it had to be done: That doesn't ease the burden.

"All the e-mails are on the machine, if you can find them. I can do that much. But understand, this had to be done."

Did it? Dr. Killian had asked himself this for weeks. And no, there was no other way out. Or was there? Was he justified? What if he was wrong? If you did something horrible that cost a few dozen lives, but thousands were saved, were you right in sacrificing the few? The math worked. Statistically, he was right. He was a scientist; he believed in facts. But he'd realized during the last few days that being logical did not exempt him from being human. He still felt guilt, and he couldn't live with that guilt any more than he could survive an interrogation.

"I'm shaking. Getting hard to type. Goodbye."

Dr. Killian sent his document to print, but made no motion to get up and walk to the printer. Best to leave it there, where it would stay clean.

He shut down his computer. Yes, he'd give them all the information they needed, but he had state-of-the-art encryption on his hard drive. That would give Extremis plenty of time to take hold, to demonstrate its awesome and innovative power and abilities, and would keep out all but the most determined hardware and software engineers. The FBI might get in after weeks of effort, but none of his colleagues would. Their brilliance was in biology and medicine, not software hacking.

This had to be done, Dr. Killian thought again. He slid open the desk drawer to his right, revealing a loaded pistol. He heard Dr. Hansen hang up the phone and swear. She threw something, and it thudded against their shared wall. The reporters were getting on her nerves. She'd be in here in just a minute, would pick up the note from the printer. Would call the paramedics from her cell phone. He'd have to do this right, so she'd be better off calling the county morgue.

He carefully released the gun's safety mechanisms, checked the magazine, and turned the barrel around. He checked the website where he'd bought the handgun one more time to confirm he'd done all this correctly, since he'd never used a gun before. He placed the barrel squarely between his eyes, then moved it into his mouth, instead, and pointed it upward. He thought about the impersonal signs on bridges back home, back east where he'd spent his formative years, the ones imploring would-be jumpers to call a telephone number rather than jumping. He'd rather have jumped back home, he thought, where he'd have ended up a paragraph buried deep in a daily tabloid rather than the subject of the front-page drama that was likely to unfold here. Blowing his brains out seemed a bit gory. He'd lived his life in this box, and he would end it here. At least he'd give some color to the drab beige cubicle, a little joke no one else would understand. His wife would have, if he'd had a wife.

"I've never been in love," he said aloud. He didn't care whether anyone heard him. In moments, nothing he'd said would matter. "Never. No one's ever loved me."

He felt warm tears rolling out of his eyes, stinging his pores as they slid down his cheeks. He'd never imagined his life would end this way, never considered such a solution before. His actions with Extremis had been necessary, of course, but he hadn't expected the guilt, or the shame. *God, the shame!* He was a respected scientist. He couldn't live with it. In time, when Extremis had been used to save lives, perhaps people would understand.

Dr. Aldrich Killian pulled the trigger.

TWO

Tony stood in front of the ten-foot-tall plate-glass window behind the oak desk in his ninth-floor office, overlooking Luna Park, the Cyclone, the boardwalk, a strip of sand, and the Atlantic Ocean beyond. He could see his fans outside the Stark Enterprises gates. Something was happening down there. They were pushing and crowding each other. Either Iron Man had just shown up—which was unlikely, since Tony *was* Iron Man—or some generous soul had just given them all free rides on the Wonder Wheel.

Mrs. Rennie will come up with something novel as revenge, Tony realized. She hated heights. With any luck, she'd be put into one of the cars that wasn't fixed to the rim. The sliding cars were perfectly safe. But that didn't mean she'd appreciate their safety record when her car suddenly careened along a rail from hub to rim.

He rather enjoyed her surliness. Not that he'd ever tell her. And he'd never tell Pepper how entertaining Mrs. Rennie was. He wanted Pepper to come back, of course. Her efficiency and competence were essential to the workings of Stark Enterprises; he wasn't sure the company could survive without her. And then there was her charm, her warmth and humor, and how stunning she looked in a low-slung, backless evening gown. Mrs. Rennie couldn't really match her on that front.

The office door opened. Tony didn't turn around. He could see his reflection—that was a nice new suit Mrs. Rennie had sent over, and he looked great in it— and behind him, two figures entering the room with a tripod and a camera. That would be the documentary team.

"Coney Island," Tony mused aloud, sweeping his right arm to indicate the panoramic view below. "My dad used to tell me this was the most fantastic place in the world. The amusements. The constructions.

"See the Parachute Jump? A steel engineering marvel of the 1939 World's Fair, New York's own Eiffel Tower. Amelia Earhart made the first jump from its precursor, and it stayed lit all through the World War II blackouts. And the Wonder Wheel? Forged on site in 1920.

"People believed they had to be living in the future, to be able to visit an incredible place like Coney Island. And at night they wouldn't go home. They'd sleep on the beach, so they could wake up here, in the future.

"They don't sleep on the beach anymore. The Parachute Jump hasn't even been in operation during my lifetime." Tony turned around. The cameraman—or camera-intern, more like it—was already setting up the tripod. His boss, a white-haired man of about sixty, looked a little older than he had in the publicity stills Tony had seen.

"I'm sorry," said Tony. "Mister Bellingham, yes?"

"John Bellingham. Thank you for your time."

"Not at all. I'm an admirer of your documentaries, Mister Bellingham. Shall we get started?"

Bellingham sat down first, using his arms to slowly lower his body into the padded guest chair in front of Tony's desk. He moved deliberately, like a man carrying a burden. Like a man who had seen many things over during the decades, and who felt those things weighing upon his entire being.

"You're very kind," said Bellingham. "Gary, you want to set up?"

Bellingham didn't take his eyes off Tony as he addressed the cameraman. Tony realized that while Bellingham's actions were mechanical and seemingly innocuous, his eyes took in everything. His mind absorbed all he was seeing. But Tony had been transparent in recent months, since he'd admitted to the world he was Iron Man. He had nothing to hide.

"I'm cool," said Gary. "So long as you stay there and Mister Stark is behind the desk. I'm going to close the blinds, though. Nice view up here." He walked to the window and swiveled his head left, then right. He looked quizzically back at Tony.

"Sorry," said Tony. He spoke into his phone. "Close blinds."

The blinds slid silently, vertically across the windows, blocking out the sun.

Tony reached across his desk to shake Bellingham's hand.

"What's the name of this film again, Mister Bellingham?"

"Ghosts of the Twentieth Century."

"Hm. Okay." Tony wasn't sure he liked the sound of that. He thought about the abandoned Parachute Jump—and about the old Thunderbolt roller coaster, once an innovative marvel, demolished as an eyesore a decade ago. What exactly was Bellingham's point?

"Ready, Gary?" Bellingham wasn't interested in Tony's hesitancy.

"Speed. In your own time, John." Gary hit the record button and nodded to Bellingham to start whenever he was ready.

Bellingham sat up straight and held a manila envelope within view of the camera.

"I'm here at the Coney Island office of Stark Enterprises with the company's founder, CEO, and head technologist, Anthony Stark," began Bellingham.

"Tony's fine."

"Tony." Bellingham stared across the desk, his lined face suddenly becoming accusing and deliberate.

"Would it be fair to define you as an arms dealer?"

Tony had anticipated this line of questioning and was ready for it. "Absolutely not. I am a social entrepreneur, and Stark Enterprises has ceased all weapons research. I admit that up until recently—"

Bellingham interrupted. "But Stark did design and sell arms for decades?"

Tony kept his expression unchanged. "I wouldn't deny that we have designed arms for the U.S. military, of course. This is well-documented."

"In fact," continued Bellingham. "It's your heritage, how you made your millions, why you can afford to step back from weapons today and still have a company. Stark Enterprises was founded on weaponeering, I believe."

"My first major contract was for the U.S. Air Force, yes."

"What was that contract?"

Tony's face stayed calm. Bellingham's line of attack, so far, was accurate and not unexpected. "My initial engineering interest was miniaturization. The USAF saw applications in munitions."

"And that was the seedpod bomb, yes?" Bellingham had done his research.

"It was the same process, however, that led to—"

"The seedpod was first used in Gulf War One? How old were you?"

Tony hadn't thought about this in years. He'd been a kid, working with DIY gear in his room at night. "I was a teenager."

"Now correct me if I'm wrong. But the seedpod dispensed hundreds of 'smart' micromunitions from a mother-bomb casing, yes?"

"As I said before, Stark no longer makes weapons, including the seedpod," said Tony. "But, yes, it was intended to destroy airfields and cripple armored convoys."

"Did it work?" Bellingham surprised Tony now. "Did all of those bomblets go off as anticipated?"

Tony thought quickly. Bellingham was presenting classified information on camera. "You'll have to ask the military. We never got an operations report on every single micromunition. There were tens of thousands—"

"Perhaps you'd like to look at these pictures." Bellingham handed over the manila envelope.

Aware that his reaction could imply much about the envelope's contents, Tony accepted and opened the folder carefully. He pulled out a group of photos and paged through them, carefully shielding the distressing images of dying and injured people from the camera lens.

"Each one of your bomblets has the explosive force of three sticks of dynamite," continued Bellingham. "Eighteen percent of them suffered time failures. They're scattered across the theater of conflict.

"Children find them, Tony."

Tony could see the cameraman zooming in on his face. He did not visibly react.

"Can you tell us what the Stark Sentinel is?" Bellingham wasn't letting up.

"It's a land mine." Of course Tony knew what it was. He'd designed it in his early twenties. The land mines formed the defensive line between North and South Korea. *What's Bellingham's point here?*

"You're unaware of Stark land mines in, say, East Timor?"

"Yes." Tony was not aware of any Stark weapons in East Timor, but he knew from his own experience that weapons had a way of showing up in unintended places. That was one of the reasons he'd quit designing them.

And he was intimately acquainted with the Stark Sentinel. That was the land mine that had nearly killed him in Afghanistan.

"Tell me about when you were injured in Kunar Province, Mister Stark. Was it an IED?"

Bellingham knew an improvised explosive device had not injured Tony in Afghanistan. *He's baiting me*, thought Tony. The tan, dry dunes and scrubby brush of the Afghan desert were vividly imprinted in his memory, as was the sight of soldiers unloading Stark Sentinel mines from armored military vehicles.

"Our convoy had stopped outside a base," he said, neglecting to answer the question. "I was consulting."

"By consulting, do you mean showing off your latest deadly inventions? Trying to sell them?"

Tony ignored the slight.

"When I looked the base up online, soldiers had posted reviews of it. 'Great place to take the family. All that's missing is a carousel.' And you should see the fake cooking-show videos they'd posted of Meals Ready to

Eat. You wouldn't believe what those guys do with jalapeno cheese spread. Our soldiers are young people making a living, patriots with families and hopes and dreams. They deserve to be protected, Mister Bellingham. And yes, I was making a great deal of money keeping them safe. But don't you see? I *did* keep them safe. Hundreds of lives were shielded from harm by Stark technology, and millions more from medical advances that evolved from that same technology."

Tony had not been in Afghanistan—looking at ways to contain insurgency, save lives, and keep the world at peace—out of the goodness of his heart. He'd gone there to make money selling a new batch of weapons to the military. He wasn't proud of this. He was brilliant, one of the smartest visionaries on the planet. So why hadn't he realized his powerful, impossible-to-duplicate weapons were uniquely lethal, and that they would tempt all but the least corruptible with their high values on the black market?

Lost in thought, he remembered the airmen he'd watched as their futures evaporated in a rush of gunfire and blood. The general next to Tony had fallen, too, his hat and cigar crumpling as he collapsed lifeless to the road, speckled with shrapnel from a rocket-propelled grenade. Land mines spilled from the truck, but Stark Sentinels were not supposed to go off on their own. They had to be set.

And then more bullets came. From where? Tony didn't have time to consider that, back during field tests, he'd failed to study the effect of bullets hitting unarmed mines. As he watched the mines targeting, exploding, all he'd had time to think about was impact, fire, dust, pain, and the warmth of his own blood spreading across his chest.

"I'm fine now, thanks." Back in the present, Tony answered the same question he always heard about his injury in Afghanistan. But Bellingham hadn't asked it.

"Was that before or after you sold the supergun to a Gulf state?"

"I'm afraid that's classified information."

"But you did design a gun with a half-mile-long barrel intended to lob tactical nuclear devices some four hundred miles?"

Tony had security clearance, but everyone who would watch this documentary did not.

"I would like to be able to comment. But I'm under restrictions on that subject."

"I see," said Bellingham. "How many of these devices led you to the design of the 'Iron Man' suit?"

Ah, now Tony saw where Bellingham was going. This whole interview was about Iron Man. About demonizing his most brilliant invention.

"All tools have destructive potential." Tony picked up a pen and notebook to idly sketch the Iron Man armor. He jotted down a new idea: a way to use window glass to capture sounds via a laser array in the chest plate. Then he looked back up. "The repulsor has applications for cheap, non-chemical space launch." He'd been thinking about that for a while, but Stark's new lack of military funding had limited his ability to research.

"I see. And are you developing that?"

"Not at this time." Tony stopped sketching and scratched his chin. He was committed to Stark Enterprises' new mission. But for all his genius, he couldn't work out how to make peace-for-profit more financially rewarding than war profiteering.

"The Iron Man armor is just another defense-industry application, isn't it? You use it for special-response peacekeeping, like with the Avengers. But that's just privatized defense. You've just made a new defense application, right?"

"My point—and I don't want to talk over you, John, but you're not giving me credit for anything good that's come out of our past military funding— my point, John, is that Stark microelectronic breakthroughs have all led to useful social technologies *after* they were initially funded by military research."

Tony pointed angrily across the table. "No, I didn't first think to myself that taking microchips down to the nanometer limit would be good for bombs. But that's how we made the money to expand our research, and the money from seedpod was driven into biometric medicine and internal analgesic pumps. I'm not involved in weapons design now. But yes, I was. And I question every day whether that was the right call, to make bombs in exchange for medical advances."

Bellingham sat back and crossed his arms.

"Do you think they have your painkilling drug pumps in Iraq? Do you think an Afghan kid with his arms blown off by a land mine is remotely impressed by an Iron Man suit?"

Tony sat quietly for a moment. He'd been wrestling with this for weeks now, wondering whether one injured child was too many.

"I never claimed to be perfect," said Tony quietly. "Yes, there is blood on my hands. But I'm trying to atone…Iron Man is the future. I'm trying to improve the world."

"Improve the world. Right. Thanks for your time." Bellingham stood up. Gary hit the pause button on the camera, then stop. He collapsed the tripod.

Bellingham spoke again to Tony. "I'm curious, actually. If you know my work— clearly, I was going to give you a hard time—why did you agree to this interview?"

"Me first," said Tony. "Why am I a ghost of the twentieth century?"

"Because your earlier arms work still haunts the poverty- and war-stricken countries it was deployed in."

"I wanted to meet you," Tony explained. "You've been making your investigative films for what, twenty years now? I wanted to ask: Have you changed anything? You've been uncovering disturbing things all over the world for two decades. *Have you changed anything?*"

Bellingham stood in silence. He was used to asking the hard questions, not answering them.

"You've worked very hard. Most people have no idea of the kind of work you've done. Intellectuals, critics, and activists follow your documentaries closely. But culturally, you're almost invisible, Mister Bellingham."

Tony stood directly in front of the filmmaker.

"Have you changed anything?"

Bellingham thought for a moment, then answered honestly.

"I don't know."

"Me neither," said Tony. "It's been an honor to meet you, Mister Bellingham." Tony was sincere. Bellingham hadn't made the interview easy on him, but he did admire the man's dogged determination to make a difference in the world.

"Yes, thank you for your time, Mister Stark."

Bellingham and the cameraman walked away. Tony thought for a minute about going back to sleep— but no, he had a world to defend, even without Stark's weapons. He turned his back to the door and picked up his phone.

"Open blinds."

The light streamed back in, revealing the glorious view of Coney Island and the Atlantic. Coney Island had been reinventing itself since Ulysses S. Grant was in the White House. Tony could do the same: revitalize Stark Enterprises and engineer a better world.

He could be the test pilot for the future.

Mallen could no longer sense the damp stickiness of his own blood on the slaughterhouse floor, no longer feel the chill of sweat. He was aware only of a throbbing headache, faint nausea, and the vague tingling of his stiff, unmoving limbs. He lay where he'd collapsed after the injection, unable to see anything aside from the swollen cheeks below his eyes and his own right hand stretched out in front of him. He was covered in fatty, swirled masses of copper-colored scar tissue, nearly alien in appearance. He saw all this through a haze of red, as if his eyes themselves had turned magenta.

He faded in and out of dizzy consciousness—one moment aware of his prone state, the next deliriously hallucinating. He saw his first foster father, in a rush of memory mixed with nightmare, lying stiff just as Mallen did now, unmoving on the trailer floor among the whisky bottles. Mallen flashed to a social worker then, a tired woman wearing too much eye shadow and concealer, suddenly noticing young Mallen when he asked why his foster father was dead so often.

He remembered a kind older couple. They were a blur of pancakes for dinner and swinging on a porch, but one of them had gone to the emergency room and never come back. Then the red haze came again, and he felt the pain of past beatings with the piercing spasms in his evolving organs. From older kids and teachers, from angry foster fathers when he'd fight… when he'd steal…when he refused to be polite to guests. As he'd gotten older, he started hitting back, especially when the younger kids would get punished. Then he'd get sent back to the county shelter, where he'd fight again. Later there had been military school, but he'd been quickly expelled, returned to the county shelter after he'd taken a sink off the boys' bathroom

wall with a medieval mace purchased at an online replica shop.

Mallen had liked the idea of military school, of still
having a chance at making something of himself, but
they wouldn't give him a gun. He'd just wanted a rifle,
like when he was a kid and his dad would take him to
the turkey shoot set up every year by the fire-depart-
ment volunteers.

Mallen had never hit the target, much less won.
But his dad had won—not just the turkey, but all kinds
of prizes: slabs of bacon, hunting knives, cider. His
mother, too, would win. She'd show him her targets,
pointing out how close she'd been. He hadn't understood at first. Why was she shooting a target instead of
a turkey?

Mallen felt a cramp in his leg, but he couldn't
move. When he'd gone deer hunting with his dad, he'd
had to sit unmoving for hours, making no sound. But
this…this wasn't hours. How long had he been here
now? Days?

He was imprisoned by his body, no longer recog-
nizable as his own—trapped by a bio-metallic cocoon.
He was *incubating*. Transforming. But into what?

THREE

Iron Man saves lives.

Tony thought about the interview with Bellingham as he headed out of his office to the elevator. He was in the business of helping the world, not harming it.

Right?

His phone rang. *Mrs. Rennie, as usual.* Tony watched the phone ring, making sure the elevator camera caught him simply staring at it for a moment. Then, on the fifth ring, he finally picked up.

"How's your practicing going for the Nathan's Hot Dog Eating Contest?" he asked.

"Your fans can take care of that important task, Mister Stark. I only eat junk food when it's available on a stick." She paused, then changed the subject. "I've informed your senior staff that you're available for a meeting since you've finally emerged from that dreary garage."

"No meetings, Mrs. Rennie. I have actual real work to do."

"Running Stark Enterprises is part of your work, Mister Stark, and given that you've delegated care and feeding of your eager fans to me…"

"Later, Mrs. Rennie. Later," said Tony. He clicked the phone off. She really needed to be paying attention to the ticket seller at the Wonder Wheel box office, not lecturing him pointlessly. He was well aware of his responsibilities as CEO of Stark Enterprises.

John Bellingham says the Iron Man suit is a military application, he thought. *I told him he was wrong. Iron Man is used for extraordinary rescue-and-response situations. For helping people in trouble. Right?*

What if I was lying?

His phone rang again. The name GEOFF PETERSON popped up. He was on Stark's board of directors—a dull bureaucrat Tony had promoted out of the accounting department. Clumsy with women, though excellent with details and numbers. Tony dreaded spending time with him. *Might as well get this over with.*

"Geoff, how the heck are you? Tell me something: Does Iron Man save lives?"

"Tony, what did Bellingham get you to say on screen?"

"Nothing untrue. It went all right. We'll talk about the interview later."

"Mrs. Rennie set up a senior staff meeting at four.

And we need to update you on—"

"What? Geoff, I'm on the elevator, and you're cutting out. Get on those new Stark phones right away, we can take that market. Our satellites reach everywhere. I can't hear you. See, the world needs a Stark phone." He clicked off, chuckling. The elevator reached the ground floor, and he headed out the service entrance.

As Tony entered the garage, he tossed the phone on to the workbench. He loosened his tie, then stripped off his suit and began to speak.

"Stark voicelog: Record: Datestamp.

"Iron Man represents the future. I've never sold any element of the Iron Man armor to the military."

Naked now, Tony stood in darkness in front of his Iron Man suit. The only light was a faint glow coming from his own chest—from the embedded circular arc reactor that had saved his life and that powered his armor. The red-and-gold Iron Man armor was huge, powerful, and bulky. He'd previously fit a portable version into a briefcase, but his modifications eventually had made it too large. He hadn't worked out how to make the suit both powerful and convenient.

Tony pulled on his polymer circuit-skin first, covering himself from neck-to-toe. This flexible substrate film of microscopic physiological conductors was designed to interact via miniaturized sensor units with the armor on his wireless body area network, or WBAN. The armor needed to be able to act almost as his limbs, to respond at the speed of thought. Anything else would put him at risk.

"That land mine put shrapnel two centimeters from my heart," Tony continued, still recording his voicelog. "My every movement allowed it to inch closer. I had to design a system to hold the shrapnel where it was, then incorporate that system into a self-defense solution to break me out of captivity.

"It was the first time I'd had to design something that *saved* lives."

He stepped forward into the armor, clicking it open and shut a piece at a time. The shin guards. The boots. The gauntlets. Each component snapped on methodically, in a precise order. He preferred the automated process he'd installed at both the Midtown corporate center and at the Stark West Coast headquarters, but out here at Coney Island, Tony had to put on the suit manually.

"It was a stopgap measure, but it got me home. I've improved it, tinkered with it, ever since. I wasn't sure why at first—except that it wasn't about *the* future, but *my* future. The armor allows me to pretend I'm not just a man who made land mines. The reactor, the armor—it keeps me alive. I'm not a man trapped in armor. I'm a man freed by it."

He pulled the helmet over his head. Tony Stark was now completely covered in advanced technology, decades ahead of any other system on the planet. He flipped the visor down, transforming his look from human to machine.

"Iron Man command system on. Start."

Iron Man's chest-plate arc reactor and eyes glowed

white. Inside the armor, Tony glanced at the readouts on his internal helmet holographic display. The word *LOADING* appeared.

"Root/experimental systems/ocular motion reader for sight-based system control. Start."

Propulsion and repulsor levels steadily rose to capacity.

"Launch."

Iron Man's boot jets emitted a fiery kinetic thrust, propelling him upward in a haze of non-toxic emissions. He rose slowly, then sped up. He glanced at the garage roof and watched his target crosshairs lock on it. Nice to see ocular targeting was online, but blasting his way out of the garage wasn't necessary. "Targeting systems off," said Tony, as steel roof doors on motion sensors slid aside, opening a portal from the garage to the outside world.

After weeks of seclusion, Iron Man rocketed into the blue sky of a bright Brooklyn afternoon. Dozens of heads down below looked up, all at once. Iron Man—at heart a showman, like his father Howard Stark before him—did a somersault, lost balance for a second, then waved cheerily at the crowd below. He blew a kiss to his fans.

"Recalibrate mobility control, Jarvis," Tony said, speaking to the AI-enhanced supercomputer that was the backbone of his Iron Man suit. Tony concentrated on the visual flight system interface—the HUD, or Heads-Up Display, which projected holographic information within his line of sight. "Set stability to automatic for the next two minutes. I'm out of practice."

"Certainly, sir." Tony had programmed his AI with the attributes of his former butler, Edwin Jarvis, once employed by Tony's father and now head of the Avengers' support staff. Like Jarvis himself, Tony's AI was usually efficient—but unlike the flesh-and-blood butler, the AI wasn't always good with subtext or subtlety.

He flew in low, low enough to see slack-jawed strangers mouthing the words "Iron Man" and "He's the coolest" as he streaked above them on his way to the beach, leaving vapor trails all the way to the Atlantic. He shot straight up, broke the sound barrier, gained altitude, then hovered as he checked his readings. All were normal.

"Ha ha ha ha ha!" Tony had been inside too long. That interview with Bellingham had given him renewed faith in his mission and in Stark Enterprises' new direction. He flew now because he could, because he wanted to believe in himself. He'd made all this possible through engineering, his conviction that a better future lie ahead, and his own innate genius.

"Jarvis, run plasma diagnostics. Confirm that all cybernetics and the cooling system are at one hundred percent. Do a complete check. The suit has been in mothballs too long."

As he awaited the report from the systems check, Tony gazed at the brilliance of the afternoon—at the roiling sea, the living past, its ecosystem billions of years old. Then he looked over at a jumble of the present and hope for the future, miracles of human engineering and innovation, the Verrazano Bridge and the amusements of Coney Island.

He could hear the screams of thrill-seekers as they rattled along the Cyclone roller-coaster tracks, just as they had since 1927. The screams competed with the thumping bass from the speakers of a dance party on the dizzying Polar Express ride, and the crack of a baseball bat at the park that had helped revitalize the area yet again after years of ups and downs, once more moving it forward into the future.

Tony listened for the screams of the riders on the Wonder Wheel. *No screams,* he thought. Something was wrong.

The Wonder Wheel at Luna Park was motionless. All lights and power had been cut. That never happened. Well, almost never. Only during giant blackouts or storms affecting the entire coastline. "Open a line to Mrs. Rennie," said Tony.

A minute later, her voice filled his helmet. "Hurry, Mister Stark. A foolish teenager climbed out of one of the Wonder Wheel passenger cars while the ride was moving. They've stopped the ride now, but he's hanging from the car and seems likely to fall. Your fans are not enjoying this. Also, a child has vomited on my shoes."

"Cease diagnostics, Jarvis."

"Cooling systems are offline for testing. Minimum reboot time is eighteen seconds. Using repulsor systems without cooling is not recommended."

"Eighteen seconds is too long. Keep cooling offline. I'll hurry."

Iron Man hesitated just long enough for processing to cease, then blasted through the air back to Coney Island.

How and why had a teenager gotten out of the Wonder Wheel carriage? A dare? A suicide attempt? A hazing? You don't figure out how to unlock a sliding cage door at 150 feet by accident. But there was no time to speculate. Iron Man zoomed across the surf and sand, over the boardwalk, past the kiddie park, and came in low beneath the Ferris wheel. Tony mentally calculated the trajectory of the boy, if he should fall.

"Jarvis, how hot am I?" For the moment, Tony was glad to have not built his butler's sense of humor into the suit's AI.

"Within acceptable parameters. You have ten seconds until you will begin to sweat profusely. In approximately two minutes, you risk serious dehydration. Experimentation beyond that point is not recommended. The Iron Man suit's composite alloy has not been tested for suitability in baking or roasting situations."

"Send a message to Happy—tell him to meet me at the Wonder Wheel with a smoothie, and make a note for me to try cooking brownies in this thing one day."

As Tony approached the Wonder Wheel, he spotted the teen clinging precariously to an open carriage door. The kid had had the bad fortune to board one of the red cars that swings wildly along a track along with the Wheel's movements. Any motion could send the carriage sliding along the rail, taking the kid with it.

Iron Man slowed to hover just beneath the car.

"Let's go, kid. Just take your hands off the rail. I'm going to catch you and put you back in the car."

"Not back in the car!" The teen's eyes were wide. He looked terrified.

"Um, okay. Not back in the car. We'll go to the ground. Ground is good." Tony fired off the smallest possible repulsor thrust and gently rose through the air to hover alongside the kid. He was sizzling inside the armor, which threatened to overheat. This had to end quickly.

"N-n-n-nooo!" The teenager wasn't going to make this easy.

"Look, kid, you can't stay here forever. You'll get hungry. You'll need to go to school. You'll have to go to the bathroom. You've got to convince yourself to let go so I can help you. You're in charge of your muscles. Take over. I get that this was probably an unexpected turn to your day, but you are strong enough to let those muscles know who's boss."

"I…I can't."

"Kid, I understand. I know right now I look tough in all this fancy armor, but once, when I was about your age, I went SCUBA diving near San Diego with my… well, my dad's pilot. I'd like to say I went with my dad, but my dad was busy a lot, so his pilot took me. Because he didn't have all that much to do when my dad didn't need to fly somewhere. And I didn't know what I was doing—I had no business even trying to dive, didn't have a license—but sometimes when you're rich, people overlook things like licenses. Worse, you make stupid decisions. And I got into some trouble, so I just grabbed the ship's anchor line, and bobbed up and down, up and down in the waves—afraid to go under and afraid to let go. I thought I was going to drown out there in the ocean, and I'd get eaten by a walrus or something. But I had to let go, or else no one could pull me up and on to the boat."

"Did you…did you let go?"

"Yeah, I did. But only after the captain stuck his head over the railing and told me, like I'm pointing out to you, that if I didn't let go, he couldn't help me. He said if I let go, the waves would carry me up to the front of the boat, and he'd catch me. He said I had to trust him."

The kid started to relax, finally.

"I'll try."

Suddenly, a teenage girl stuck her head out from inside the car.

"I didn't think he'd take it so bad. Wait, you're Tony Stark under that metal, aren't you? The handsome billionaire? Want to go get some pizza after this?" She smiled and giggled.

"I'd climb out if I were stuck with someone as insensitive as her, too," said Iron Man quietly to the teenage boy.

The girl shifted her weight and held out an arm, positioning herself to snap a photo of Iron Man with her phone. "Move up a bit, I want to be in the picture, too," she commanded.

"Wait, don't move!"

Too late. The girl's movement sent the carriage sliding down the rail. The boy struggled to hang on to the moving car, but his grip was slipping.

The boy plummeted. Between him and the ground were more than a hundred feet of steel rails.

"Jarvis, engage overdrive."

Iron Man caught up to the teenager almost instantly, grabbing him about the waist and chest, then pulling him clear of the Wheel just before he collided with one of the main rims.

Tony decelerated on the way down, holding the frightened kid's midsection tight. They landed, a bit more abruptly than Tony intended. He was distracted by sweat rolling into his eyes.

"Jarvis, bring cooling system back online," said Tony. "And hurry. My eyes feel like they're on fire, and my vision is blurred."

"Database search recommends a moisture-wicking headband."

"Thanks, Jarvis. You're a big help." Tony pulled off his helmet, squinting and blinking as his eyes watered.

"Mister Iron Man?"

Tony made out the shape of the teenager he'd just rescued. The kid held out a bottle of water.

"Thanks. Just pour it over my head." He leaned forward while the teen flushed out his eyes. He was trying to avoid letting the water run into his circuit-skin, which was already soaked from sweat.

"You okay, kid? That wasn't real smart. She totally wasn't worth it, y'know? What's your name?"

"Well, Owen, you're young now, and you're going to look back at this someday and…"

Tony was interrupted by the shrill voice of authority. The Wonder Wheel had begun turning again, and as a car swivelled down to the ground, Mrs. Rennie climbed out.

Owen stepped back a foot. He could see he was in trouble as this diminutive but stern senior citizen briskly approached him.

"Owen, my name is Mrs. Rennie. We're going to have a discussion. You're going to tell me what exactly you were thinking, then you are calling your mother."

Tony grinned and turned away quickly, so Owen couldn't see his face.

"Sir?" Happy was on the scene now, offering Tony a smoothie. Tony grabbed it enthusiastically from his burly friend's hand, pulled off the lid, and gulped. *Mmm, mango and yogurt.* He heard a few cameras clicking, took a look at the brand name on the drink, and wondered briefly whether the Mango Mermaid company was now going to claim that Iron Man endorsed its product. *Ah, well, the legal team is busy, and Stark Enterprises supports local businesses.* He slurped the smoothie down, smiled for the cameras, pulled his helmet back on, and tossed the cup back to Happy.

"Good luck, Owen." Iron Man fired up his repulsors and roared off into the sky, soaring back to hover over the Atlantic.

"Jarvis, proceed with diagnostics. I'll just float here while you finish. Dial Pepper."

"Ms. Potts' phone is offline."

"Use the satellite server. She's out of cell-tower reach."

Pepper answered, breathless. "Tony, I can't talk. I'm about to meet a potential partner for dinner."

"Dinner? Partner?" Tony didn't like it when Pepper had plans he didn't know about. "What's his name? Did he ask you, or did you ask him? Is he single?"

"HER name. I'm allowed to eat, you know. And I've got a great lead for your project."

"I sent you to...wait, I've forgotten. It's been a long day. Which country are you in now?"

"Another place with a visa that takes up an entire page of my passport. This is my second passport in eight months."

"I'll get you a deluxe-sized passport next time, Pepper. I have connections, you know."

"You charmer. You are so smooth with the ladies. Honestly, the next time—"

Jarvis interrupted now. "Incoming call from Mrs. Rennie."

"I'm on an important call. Tell her to wait."

"Mister Stark, I'll do no such thing. I do not wait particularly well. Good evening, Ms. Potts. My best wishes for the ongoing success of your journey."

Tony really needed to work on the armor's privacy settings.

"Mister Stark, there is a Miss Maya Hansen on the line. She insists you will take her call regardless of whatever flying escapades you might currently be involved in. She says you made her this promise. In a bar. Over drinks."

Pepper cleared her throat and hung up. Mrs. Rennie chuckled evilly as Tony sighed. She'd gotten him back for all the fun he'd had with her this morning. In spades.

Score one for Mrs. Rennie, he thought.

"Patch her through," said Tony.

FOUR

"Tony?"

"Maya! This is a surprise. What've you been up to? It's been a while."

"Years, Tony. I saw you on the news. Looks like you've been busy. Like you've made some progress on miniaturizing repulsor tech. Remember our deal from Techwest? We promised to take each other's calls and IMs. Always."

"Was this the deal we made at that lousy bar under the influence of beer you convinced me someone else had already digested and passed?"

"Yes. Twice. Look, I know this seems out of the blue, but I really need to talk to you. Something's happened here, and...well, it feels like the last straw."

"Where is here, Maya?"

"I'm at my desk, at Futurepharm. The main labs. Outside Austin."

"Why me? Is this something for Iron Man?"

"It's classified, Tony. Biomedical engineering. You have security clearance, and no one else will understand what's gone wrong."

"There's Sal."

"He's off-grid in Sonoma County. I know he's a genius with biotech, but you have the benefit of owning a phone. It's an emergency, Tony. I need *you*."

Tony glanced at his armor's readings, and then looked backward and down at his office building on Coney Island. It was great to be out of the garage, great to be flying. He'd fly all day if he could, and heading to Texas would give him that opportunity. But he had a business to run, and he didn't want to attend a Stark Enterprises board meeting from inside the armor. He quickly made up his mind.

"See you in a few hours. I'll bring the jet."

"Aren't *you* a jet?" Maya started to giggle, but it turned into a cough—or was that a sob? Tony remembered Maya as a flirty, brilliant scientist, but she sounded like she had a lot more than flirtiness on her mind.

"We might want to visit a few wineries. Or pick up a sandwich."

"I heard you don't drink anymore. But yeah, fine. Bring the jet. And Tony?" She paused just long enough to make him feel uncomfortable. "It'll be good to see you."

"You, too, Maya. Be there soon."

Tony clicked off the phone and switched back to Mrs. Rennie's direct line.

"Have the staff ready the new jet at JFK. I'm uploading the GPS routing for the flight path. The Iron Man suit comes with me, just in case, but this is a Tony Stark expedition."

"Well, obviously, or you'd just fly there yourself and save us some money. Have you forgotten your senior staff meeting this afternoon?"

"Enable teleconferencing on the plane. Send Happy into my garage to get my overnight bag and that nice suit you picked out for me. Give him anything Geoff wants me to review for the meeting. I'll meet Happy at the airport. And another thing, Mrs. Rennie."

"What now, Mister Stark?"

"Thanks for helping with that kid, Owen."

"You're welcome, but you must never deliberately place me in the line of fire of funnel cake again. I detest fried foods."

"Unless it's on a stick."

"Unless it's on a stick," agreed Mrs. Rennie. She let out a rare peal of laughter, surprising Tony. He wasn't used to hearing her admit she enjoyed anything. "Now, then, who is this Maya Hansen?"

"An old...er...friend," said Tony. "A very smart friend."

"A word of unsolicited advice, Mister Stark. When you first hired me, you asked if I 'had an eye on the future or carried the past around like it was my own armor.' I answered correctly, because I wanted the job and it was clear to me which answer you were looking for. Now it's your turn. Don't forget to leave the past where it belongs. Your intention may be to help a friend, but Maya Hansen did not sound particularly business-formal to me. I distinctly heard her flirt with you. Shall I ask Ms. Potts if she noticed the same?"

"I, uh, I'll ask her myself. You really don't have to. I've gotta go. A flock of Canadian geese are heading my way, and I'm in their flight path. Listen, do you hear them? Well, you would if I could hold the phone out. But it's built into my armor. They sound like this. *Squawk. Squawk.*" He increased the volume and used his ocular controls to add a bit of distortion.

"Don't fly over the wildlife refuge, Mister Stark," Mrs. Rennie reminded him as she clicked off.

Tony had plenty of time, even if he circled around Jamaica Bay Wildlife Refuge. The airport was only fifteen miles away, and one advantage of being Iron Man was he didn't have to fight traffic.

Just birds, thought Tony, as he soared the long way around the refuge, out over the Atlantic.

Maya Hansen had sounded exhausted and shaken on the phone—not happy-go-lucky as she had been when they'd first met, when she'd teased him from the end of the bar at Techwest. When had that been? Ten years ago? More?

"I swear, you're the only one here in a suit. Makes you look twenty years older," Maya had said from two barstools away. She'd been wearing faded jeans and a tight baby-doll tee silkscreened with a Pi symbol. Her hair had been short then, a brown tousled pixie cut.

"I'm here to work," Tony had said stiffly. He'd been going through a phase of being far too serious. "I run a corporation."

"The rest of us are here to talk, you know. We love to talk." Maya smiled at him over her drink. What had she been drinking that night? He couldn't remember. It wasn't beer. The beer had come later, once Sal had joined them.

"Yeah. I kind of worked that out. Lots and lots of talk." At that age, Tony had lacked patience when it came to polite conversation. "Talking about repurposing robot vacuum cleaners for military work. Talking about consumer satellite telephony. God."

Maya's demeanor had changed. Apparently, she didn't like being judged.

"You don't like talking?" Maya's voice took on a menacing edge.

"I like talking about things that'll work," answered Tony. "I like talking about genuine outbreaks of the future. Not vacuum-cleaner death machines and satellite phones no one will buy or care about.

"Why does it have to be about consumer goods? Why do we assume the future is only a retail opportunity? I dunno. It bugs me."

Maya smiled again, her dimples making her all the more adorable. She scooted over to the barstool next to Tony.

"You're weird." She poked him in the chest.

"What?" Tony wasn't used to that response from women. Or anyone.

"Look at you," said Maya. "Barely out of your twenties. In a suit at a future-of-technology conference. A suit! Do you even realize this is the Bay Area? And you complaining about consumer society, as if you're better than that. Meanwhile, *you* got your money from the military."

"You know who I am?"

"*Everyone* here knows who you are."

"Huh. I shouldn't be surprised. I *am* famous—and fascinating, of course. But you're the first person who's said two words to me here."

"They're terrified of you," Maya explained. "You reinvented microtechnology in your dad's garage. Your brain is like three feet over the heads of everyone else here. Or anywhere, I guess. You're Tony Stark." She stuck out her hand. "I'm Maya Hansen."

"The medical designer? Reprogramming the repair center?" Dr. Maya Hansen was much younger and cuter than Tony had imagined her to be. She stood up, glancing at the watch embedded in her black leather wristband.

"Right. Hey, Sal Kennedy's about to talk. You want to come see it with me?"

Tony didn't know who Sal Kennedy was, but he was ready to go anywhere this cute pixie with a superbrain asked him to. "Who's he?"

"Kennedy? Started out as a computer guy. Became

an ethnobotanist, then learned lots about biotech. Works as a futurist now."

"Sounds like it'd at least be interesting," Tony lied. "Maybe he'll tell us how to make a satellite phone out of a robot vacuum cleaner."

Maya grabbed him by the hand. "So come on. And loosen your tie."

For the first time since the injection two days ago, Mallen felt a faint breeze brush past his shoulder. He shivered and pulled his tan leather coat closer, using it as a blanket. He was naked now, under the coat. His skin was tough, slightly bronze-tinted, and covered in blotches of dried blood and mucus.

Where had his clothes gone? He remembered a haze of fever and pain. He'd stripped them off in a panic, believing the clothes to be part of the scarred cocoon he'd begun to develop overnight. The room had been red then, as if he were seeing it through a mist of blood. He'd been disoriented, confused, and outraged at the surge of pain coursing along his neural pathways.

Mallen had leapt to his feet, screeching like a terrified hyena, and pounded the steel cold-room doors furiously. They'd bent beneath his alien-looking fists, shuddered when he'd thrown his scaly, evolving body up against the hinges. But the bolt had held. As they'd planned, Nilsen and Beck had locked Mallen in when they'd left him, not knowing the effects of the serum they'd just injected into their friend. Would he still be alive when they returned? Would they find a puddle of oozing goo, Mallen sleeping off the effects of the serum, or a uniquely evolved life form?

The scarred cocoon had softened and disintegrated, revealing new skin underneath—and inside that, a man who was now more than human. Mallen felt stronger, tougher, more focused, and ready to change the world. He felt heat in his throat and blood coating his teeth. He'd evolved, left weak humankind behind.

No one could take away Mallen's firearms now. He didn't need guns anymore. He was a powerful, walking weapon, stronger than guns or bombs or land mines.

The breeze hit his face. A door to the outside had opened somewhere in the slaughterhouse.

Mallen heard footsteps. Had his hearing improved, or was it just that the slaughterhouse had been silent for days? No. All his senses were sharper. He could smell his friends. Nilsen was more pungent than Beck, probably didn't shower quite as often.

Muffled voices were approaching the cold room. The lock on the door slid aside. There was Beck, fists clenched from tension and nervousness, looking apprehensive under his baseball cap. Nilsen walked in behind Beck, swinging both battered doors open wide. The two men glanced at each other and then at Mallen, who lay curled up under his coat on a stain of dried blood in the middle of the floor.

"I'm alive," said Mallen.

......

"**S**al Kennedy just might be a lunatic," Tony said, musing aloud as he snacked on a handful of bar peanuts after the Westech panel.

"Some people say the same thing about you," Maya replied icily. "Bartender, another scotch and soda, please."

"He started by claiming that nuclear plants are inevitable to the future of powering toasters in the industrialized world and ended up telling elaborate accounts of his pharmacological experiments with psychoactive dopamine inhibitors."

"That was off-topic, but he *did* answer the reporter's question."

"I was impressed with the scope of his presentation," Tony admitted. "I'm not saying he's wrong, exactly, but his projections of the future hinge on factors that are definitely going to evolve. I'm working on solutions that will change how we power our future, Maya. He's so damn certain that nothing will change. That people can't change."

"They can't. They don't," Maya said brusquely.

"He's wrong about that, Maya, and *you* are wrong about that. I'm going to alter the factors. Sal Kennedy will be stuck doing bar tricks for acolytes while I change the playing field."

"His bar tricks are just to loosen up the audience, Tony. No one in that room really believed he could mentally see inside a lemon, even if he is an ethnobotanist. This is a science conference, after all."

"Even I can do that trick," Tony said. "Bartender, do you have a whole lemon I could borrow?"

The bartender, a chestnut-haired college-age woman in a wool short-sleeve sweater and white-streaked jeans, offered up a whole lemon. "You'll give this back to me, right? Promise you won't squish my lemon."

Maya intervened, grabbing the lemon out of the bartender's hand. "Tony, *no.*" She glanced at the stem end of the lemon for a second and quickly counted the tiny sections in the stem.

"Ten. There are ten segments in this lemon. See? I can do it, too. Now cut it open and check." She shoved the lemon back at the bartender.

"No," the bartender said, looking irritated as she put the lemon away behind the bar. "You two want to prove how smart you are to each other, do it some other way. Not using my lemon."

"Fine, give me a glass and a match," said Tony. "If I can't be a citrus psychic, I'll show you my mastery of telekinesis."

"You're not smarter than I am, Tony," said Maya. "There's no bar trick you can show me that I won't be able to explain within five seconds."

"Watch." He pulled a plastic pen and two coins out of his shirt pocket. He placed one coin flat on the bar, stood the other on top of it, and then balanced the match on top of the two coins. He then put a glass over the whole setup.

"May I borrow your sweater for a moment?" Tony leaned over the bar and rubbed his pen on the bartender's sweater.

"Sure. Let me know if you need me to come closer."

Maya glared at the bartender.

Tony stood back, then circled the glass with the pen. Inside, the match pivoted with the motion of the pen.

"See? My magic powers are making the match move," said Tony.

"Sure, if by magic powers you mean static electricity, super-genius," said Maya. "Try it again, but this time rub it on my T-shirt, instead." She leaned forward.

"If you insist."

Tony moved in close to Maya and rubbed the pen on her shoulder. "Oh, sorry, Maya. Not enough real estate there. Your sleeves are too short. Mind if I…"

"You are *so* weird."

He'd moved his hand to her stomach. "This little midriff-exposing thing. Too much skin, not enough cloth. I'm going to have to move my hand up just a little higher, find the right combination of T-shirt material over a broad canvas." He'd moved his hand slowly up her ribcage, stopping just below her breasts. "How about here?"

"Like a true scientist. Finding the best solution."

"Maya, I'm not sure this is going to work. I really need something wool. How about we go see if you have something made of wool in your hotel room? I think I read in the hotel brochure that the beds have wool blankets."

"We'll have to hurry. I told Sal we'd meet him here in the bar in half an hour."

"You have an alarm on that watch, don't you?"

Tony smiled as Maya slipped off the barstool and headed toward the elevator. He turned to follow, but stopped first to hand the glass back to the bartender.

She slipped him her phone number on a ripped napkin. He winked, and turned away to follow Maya up to her room.

FIVE

"We had the new handset couriered to JFK with Happy. You have it there?" Geoff, from Stark Enterprises' board of directors, spoke for the group of five men and women around the conference room table back at headquarters.

"Yeah, Geoff," said Tony, speaking in the direction of the videoconference screen. He idly turned over the smartphone he'd found sitting on the desk of his plane's mobile office. *Looks like a phone*, he thought, *but it's clunkier, and the casing is too generic.* Geoff and his engineering team had no style. "Listen, I have notes on an ocular control system. It's partly how I run the Iron Man suit."

"Tony…"

"It's a spray of very low-power lasers that read

changes of motion and pressure in the eye. Basically, it can tell what you're looking at. Jarvis knows what Iron Man's about to ask before I say it."

"The phone, Tony." The other four board members looked blank and emotionless next to Geoff. They'd put on their best poker faces, trying not to let Tony know that they were unhappy with his decision earlier in the year to cease military contracting. Trying not to let on, yet, that they were siding with Geoff over their CEO.

Tony realized his long disappearance into the Coney Island garage probably hadn't helped the situation.

"Yeah. This is the Stark 99?" Tony turned the phone on. He made another mental note: He couldn't see the screen while sitting next to the plane window. He pulled down the window shade. *Add anti-glare screen,* he typed into the note-taking function of the phone, trying out the onscreen keyboard. If this phone had ocular controls, he realized, he could eliminate typing so long as he held the phone directly in his line of sight. *Send memo to engineering test department, re: ocular keyboard,* Tony typed. *Also, test projection keyboard with ocular use.* The responsiveness of the existing keyboard was adequate, if clunky. He liked the edge-to-edge screen, the fingerprint unlocking, and the waterproofing, but this phone had been rushed. *Why did those idiots use plastic? Anti-glare glass wasn't invented this morning.*

"You've been out of touch. We're calling it the Stark Beam 01 now. We agreed with you to build in messaging functions that circumvent network settings. Phone companies will hate us, but there are a lot more consumers than there are phone companies. Your test handset there has a special stage of functionality. It connects directly to the Stark Zipsat Constellation."

Tony considered the five executives around the tremendous wooden table in the conference room, as seen on the plane's monitor. He smiled, just a little. Some of his directors had ended up on the board through corporate acquisitions or management expertise and, like Geoff, were lacking in what Tony thought of as Stark style. But the hardware engineers working on the guts of Stark products were truly visionary.

"It has satellite Internet access?" He was marveling at this ugly little plastic device now.

"Once we—well, I mean, Iron Man makes a few adjustments to the motherboard on the main Zipsat satellite, yes. The mobile will have Zipsat broadband access, faster than any phone network. You can stream *Seven Samurai* in less time than it takes to hit the 'buy' button. Or download an entire season of *Billionaire Boys and Their Toys* in thirty seconds."

"You're all right, Geoff. Do you have a plan for getting me up to the Zipsat, or do I need to work that out myself?"

"Mrs. Rennie negotiated complimentary passage for you this afternoon on a suborbital space flight with Galactic FLX Inc. You'll be positioned at the upper edge of the mesosphere. You're on your own to get to the thermosphere from there."

"Mrs. Rennie is quite the negotiator," said Tony,

truly impressed. Getting a last-minute seat in a private space-launch wasn't easy.

"She had leverage. You've agreed to autograph 1,750 Iron Man photos for the Rocket FLX Com staff. You leave in fifty-two minutes from McGregor, Texas. Happy loaded your specialized space armor on to the plane alongside your regular armor."

Tony glanced down long enough to shoot off a text to Maya. *Might be a few minutes late, have to run an errand for work.*

Tony looked back at the screen. "What other surprises does this phone hold for me?"

"You can also hook it up to any computer, wirelessly or tethered. Click on settings and you'll see options for different operating systems…"

"If we had ocular control, we wouldn't need to click on settings," muttered Tony. Geoff ignored him and kept talking.

"This phone is going to storm the consumer end of the market, once we make a deal with a telecom company."

"Who's going to want to make a deal with us if we don't need them for half the functions on our phone?"

"That's a sticking point," Geoff admitted.

"Buy a telecom company, then."

"Tony, we're running low on funds. Your little televised stunt with the military contracts halted all our projected revenue streams for the next decade. Why do you think we got you a seat on a space launch instead of sending you up on your own plane? Which brings me to just one more thing."

"Oh, come on, Geoff. Don't start again."

"We understand that Stark needs new revenue. We're willing to work on new projects, forget the weapons, even though the weapons funding made it possible for us to advance the causes of science, engineering, and chemical research. But a CEO needs to be in his office."

"I have to go to Austin. An old friend needs me."

"You know that's not what we're talking about. It's Iron Man, Tony. He keeps you busy—search and rescue, crime-fighting, on call with S.H.I.E.L.D. and the Avengers. But we all know there's no Stark Enterprises without you. And there's also no Stark without you tinkering in your garage. You know that phone would be done already if you'd been involved. And it wouldn't be so ugly either. The engineers are good, but they're not Tony Stark."

Tony slid the plane's window shade back up so Geoff couldn't see him roll his eyes in the glare of the sun. *Don't I pay these people?* he thought. *How come they're telling me what to do?*

He pushed the "intercom" button on his armrest. Time for lunch, and he'd spotted a couple of sandwiches on the passenger seat when Happy had driven the car on board. That mango smoothie was a distant memory.

Geoff was still talking.

"Taking a Chief Technologist role doesn't remove your control. But it'll let someone else run the company."

"You think I trust someone else not to take on military contracts again?" Tony let the board see him roll his eyes this time.

"You still design for S.H.I.E.L.D., Tony."

"Not weapons. Tracking devices. Safety equipment. Rescue vehicles. It's different." Tony held the Stark Beam 01 up to the monitor. "We've just invented the best cell phone on earth. We don't need military money anymore."

The staff sat quietly on the other end, back in New York. They all looked down, shuffled papers nervously. Those papers probably showed them some unpleasant numbers that supported Geoff's concerns. Tony had seen the numbers, too. He'd even worked some of them out. That didn't change his core beliefs.

After a minute, Geoff spoke again. Tony could see that his fists were clenched, and the other board members were still intently studying the top of the conference room table.

"Tony, we're hip-deep in research and development on thirty different projects. Eighty percent of which won't realize any money in the next three years. Military money is the easiest way to improve cash flow."

"Give me another solution, Geoff. All I'm hearing from you is regret that it's no longer the past, that we can't do something we used to do. Look, it's very simple. We don't do that anymore. No more military money. Stop clinging to the past. Tell me about the future. Our future. All I am hearing is *can't can't can't*. Tell me something we *can* do."

"Okay, we could license technologies elsewhere. But we need you to sign off on those. And when you spend six weeks in the garage…"

"We can't license out. Our tech being exclusive and unique is what gives us our mystique and our edge. Besides, if we let others use our tech, they'd just do the same things we used to do, but not as well. Endgame? Lots more faulty weapons going off when they shouldn't. Stark-clone munitions destroying the unindustrialized world. I'm not prepared to be responsible for that."

"Then I don't know what to tell you, Tony. If you want to make the world a better place, you have to let someone help you. We're trying to give you ideas here, and you're not helping us. Even Bill Gates—"

"Stark is unique among corporations, and I do not look to other businessmen for guidance on how to run my company. Find me other solutions. Talk to Markko in Engineering about his plasma-powered space heaters—they've got AI, and they follow you around from room to room; if you step on one, it screams as it shuts off. Talk to R&D about their progress on underwater turbines. We can replace coal *and* oil in about twenty-five years between that and our plasma power, but we need time to work out what to do about the marine life that keeps swimming into the turbines. Give me something we can work with *now*, not in three years."

Enough, thought Tony. He clicked the "off" button in his armrest and watched Geoff open his mouth to speak again just as the monitor went dark.

"Mallen, can you stand up? You're supposed to be different now. Super-powered or something, like a redneck Captain America in jeans."

Beck reached a hand down to help pull his buddy to his feet. Mallen took Beck's hand, accidentally throwing him straight to the concrete slaughterhouse floor.

"Ow. What the hell'd you do that for?" Beck sat up, rubbing his chin where it had grazed the wall.

Mallen shrugged. "Sorry. Weird. I feel…this feels real good." He stood on one leg, testing out his knee, then switched to the other. He jumped in place a few times. "Legs are good. Nothing feels sore. My right knee used to get kind of stiff and made cracking noises when I bent it. Now, nothing."

"Can you, I dunno, fly now?" Beck was standing, looking expectantly at Mallen. "Let's figure out what that shot did to you. It sure as hell didn't make you any better lookin'."

Mallen pointed his hands in the air and jumped. He landed quickly. "No, no flying."

Nilsen looked his friend up and down. "Well, you're not glowing or anything. You don't look one bit different from how you looked before. Aside from not wearing anything. Argh, my eyes are burning!"

"C'mon, we'll work your new powers out later. Let's get you some clothes and get movin'. Nilsen has some in the van," said Beck.

"What's Nilsen doing with clothes in his van?"

The larger man looked sheepish now. "I, uh, I couldn't pay the rent last week on my room. So, fine, I live in the Econoline now. Been catching up on some reading and some TV. Have you seen *Billionaire Boys*? Man, what a bunch of worthless crap. There really is such a thing as having too much money. This country is so out of whack right now, people like that so rich they have robot dogs while I can't even come up with money for a crappy boarding house." He shook his head. "It's no big deal, me livin' in the van. Gives me time to do stuff instead of looking for rent money. I showered at Beck's yesterday."

"Just like old times." Mallen chuckled. "I used to shower at Beck's back when I lived in that old shed and worked frying chicken at Rocket Dog's Snack Shack. Remember that? That time I decided I wasn't going back to the group home?"

"*Which* time you decided you weren't going back to the group home?"

Mallen ignored Nilsen's snide remark. "Back then you didn't need paperwork to get a job. You just walked in, asked if they needed help, and they hired you."

They reached the van.

Beck walked around to the far side and hopped in, pulling the door shut behind him. Mallen slid the back door open and climbed inside, while Nilsen took his usual spot in the driver's seat. Nilsen started up the van's ignition, pulling away from the slaughterhouse toward the town center.

"So long as you said you were over sixteen—which you weren't—nobody asked any questions," Beck said. "Stupid law. If you need a job and someone needs a dishwasher, it shouldn't be that hard, y'know? You don't need to be sixteen to know how to wash dishes. What's that about? And I can't even get a job now, since I don't have any ID. It's none of the Feds' business how I make money."

"When Snack Shack asked for my phone number," continued Mallen, "I gave them the number of the pay phone at the 7-11. When they called to tell me my schedule for the week, they'd get that dope dealer and he'd write the message on the inside-front cover of the Yellow Pages. What was his name? The guy with the headband and the Van Halen shirt?"

"Oh, hell, I don't remember his name," said Beck. "What do I look like, a friggin' dictionary? Like I'm a member of the Dictionary Family?"

"The Dictionary Family! They always thought they were better 'n us. Even though they lived on the same block as your grandma, drank the same water, had to share the same air as us." Mallen hadn't thought about these old times in years, and he looked forward to putting things right, making them more like they were before. It felt good to laugh with his friends. "Remember how that one girl was always walking around with library books? We'd be sitting in the yard, practicing our swearing and pitching whisky bottles at squirrels, and that little girl would go prancing by with her stack of library books. Remember the time her sister threw the bottle back into the yard and it cut Beck's head open?"

The men howled with laughter. The van drifted to the side, and Nilsen pulled the steering wheel hard to swerve back on to the road.

"I still got the scar, look here." Beck pulled his baseball cap off and parted his hair. He leaned over the back of his seat. "Remember how the cops came, and we ended up making it look so bad they took *her* downtown?"

"You gotta know how to play the cops," said Mallen, serious now. *"Deny deny deny.* They don't tell you that in library books, do they, Dictionary Family? When the cops show up, you get your story straight and say 'I didn't hit anybody.' Works every time. So long as you're consistent and your friends don't blow it on the witness stand, there's not a damn thing they can do. None of their business anyway, what you do in the yard. How the hell did it get to where you get busted for hanging out with your buds in the front yard? Hey, I wonder if any of the Dictionary Family ever did anything other than work as a salad-bar girl at Rocket Dog's Snack Shack."

"My cousin ran into the Book Girl last Thanksgiving," said Beck. "He always thought she was kinda cute. She'd give him extra refills when he brought his own cup. Let him sneak pickles from the salad bar. Said she's in New York now. Something to do with magazines or kids' books or something."

"Pretentious losers." Mallen looked disgusted. "Thought they were better than us, but Book Girl had to work right next to me at the Snack Shack back then. I used to spit in the lettuce when she was busy flirting with the customers. She had to wear that stupid T-shirt with the beagle on the firecracker. I wore whatever I wanted cuz I worked in the back. I coulda gone to New York, too, but it's everything wrong with the world today, there and in Washington. 'Sides, I wouldn't leave my buds, 'cause we're a team."

"Look, there it is," said Nilsen. He pointed at a building on a corner. "Now it's another gourmet coffee shop, like everywhere else." He shook his head. "Used to be the Snack Shack, right there. There's a ladder on the side, back by the Dumpsters. I used to climb up to the roof at night sometimes when I couldn't stand sleeping another night at the group home. It was nice to be alone once in a while."

They drove past it in a kind of reverential silence.

"Wait. I hear something," said Mallen, suddenly alert.

Beck and Nilsen listened, but shook their heads. They heard nothing.

"I think that injection fixed up my senses. I heard you guys back at the slaughterhouse before you were even inside the building. I'm sure I just heard a woman scream."

Beck stared at Mallen for a second. "Well, that lab guy that gave us the Extremis shot said it was supposed to improve your senses and make you stronger. Let's find out if it worked. Where's the scream coming from?"

"Hang a right, then go halfway down the block. I think it's near the old roller rink, over by the supermarket." Nilsen took a right. "Park," said Mallen. "Let me out. You're too slow."

Mallen jumped from the back of the van and sped off down the block. He could still hear Beck and Nilsen as he ran. He heard them as clearly as if he were still in the van with the two men.

"He's fast, and he's got super-hearing now," said Beck. "Not bad for three days spent rolling around on the slaughterhouse floor. Wonder if there's a way to make money on this."

"What, you want to have Mallen do tricks in the shopping-mall food court while you pass around a hat? The point's not to make money, dimwit. We're going to free America from its shackles."

"I get that, Nilsen, but don't we have to eat while we free America? And we can't all three live in your van, you know."

At the end of the block, Mallen found a prone woman lying on the sidewalk. She'd been carrying a grocery bag that had fallen, scattering food across the ground by her side. Mallen remembered seeing this before.

Beck and Nilsen ran up then, puffing.

"What's going on? Do you see any muggers? I'm ready, man," said Beck. "Let's get 'em."

"There weren't any muggers," said Mallen. "It's a seizure. The old lady who worked the grill at Snack Shack used to have these."

"Nilsen, put your wallet in her mouth! She might swallow her tongue," said Beck.

"If I had enough money to carry a wallet, I wouldn't have to live out of my van," answered Nilsen. "*You* put your wallet in her mouth."

"That's BS, you morons," said Mallen. He carefully rolled the woman on to her side. "No one swallows their tongue. Evolution isn't *that* stupid. Just wait. She'll be okay."

"Dude, you believe we were made out of monkeys?" Beck looked shocked now.

Nilsen glared at him. "Don't be an idiot, Beck. Try reading once in a while."

The disoriented woman opened her eyes, and Nilsen helped her sit up. She was middle-aged, with dyed-black hair that showed graying roots. She'd painted on her eyebrows with too much makeup, giving herself a semi-permanent look of surprise.

"Hello, ma'am. We're here to help you and help fix America. Bring freedom back to the land of the free."

The woman stared at Mallen, confused, as Beck and Nilsen picked up her groceries and shoved them back into the bag. Mallen listened carefully. His new, superior hearing abilities told him that Beck had cracked three eggs and squished a tomato. When Beck accidentally put something heavy on top of a banana, Mallen realized he could smell better now, too.

"Let's go," said Nilsen. "We can't hang here too long. I parked in front of a church."

"Where do you live, ma'am?"

The dazed woman didn't answer. Mallen was getting tired of being gentle and kind. He'd been hoping for a fight, so he could test his new abilities.

"I can't help you if you don't talk," growled Mallen. He turned away from the woman. "This is stupid. Let's get out of here."

He reached down and picked up the woman, slinging her over his shoulder. He took off down the block toward a park bench, her head lolling as he ran.

"Here, ma'am. Lie on this bench and you'll feel all right after a while." Her head smacked the wooden bench as he tossed her down. "Beck, did she have anything good in the grocery bag?"

"No beer, if that's what you're asking. Nilsen took the pork chops, but I don't know where he thinks he's gonna cook them. Last time I checked, the Econoline didn't come with a kitchen."

"I'm cooking it at your place, idiot. Hey, look, ten bucks just fell out of her purse."

Mallen reached down to the ground and pocketed the ten.

"Glad we could help you out, ma'am." She stared at him, silently. He shifted uncomfortably, wondering why this woman he'd helped wasn't more grateful. "Uh, God bless America."

They left her on the bench and drove away into the night.

SIX

"Are you ready, Mister Stark? The Tavares X-2 space plane is heading back in your direction in 20 minutes. That gives you about three minutes to finish up there if you want a lift back to the stratosphere."

"Got it, Hudson. I'll jet down to the rendezvous point at the three mark. Thanks for the update." Tony's voice always sounded odd in his Mark II space armor, even though he'd added the faint hum of constant white noise after learning, on previous expeditions, how quiet space was.

Tony cut off the mic built into his airtight hood with a directed glance at his HUD and noticed an alert flashing: The software inside the space armor needed updating. The Mark II had always been more finicky than his other armors, because it was so specialized.

"Jarvis, send command to laptop to issue a reminder next time I enter my password back at Coney Island. Command: Remember to synchronize software across all armors." Then he turned back to the Zipsat satellite in front of him.

Tony had already manually reconfigured the satellite's motherboard with several jumpers he kept in his armor's waist-level tool compartment. He'd been about to replace the seals on the motherboard's protective skin when he'd had a brainstorm. After cannibalizing some of the miniaturized robotic arms from an unused expansion bay, he wired them into the motherboard with a jumper, and started ripping out the video mechanism and an LED from his new Stark Beam 01.

I need a remote satellite-update system way more than I need a flashlight or video camera on my phone, he thought. Tony enjoyed flying into space, but updating from the ground seemed a more practical strategy for future alterations to the Zipsat network.

Tony hadn't brought along a space-welding kit, so he used a chemical adhesive to melt the added components into place. *Careful,* he thought. *Don't want to end up glued to the Zipsat.*

He finished quickly—this was routine, aside from the complication of being 250 miles above the Earth's surface—and double-checked his work.

Nice job, Stark, he thought. He used his armor cameras to store images of the exact setup he'd left behind on the motherboard, then closed up the satellite. He flipped the main power switch on the Zipsat, rebooting the software and turning communications back on.

"Jarvis, use Stark Beam 01 to call Engineering. Send all video and photo records of the new Zipsat updates to Markko. Confirm receipt."

"Transmission complete, Mister Stark."

Excellent. The Zipsat was online and working.

"Try voice feature. Open a line to...try Pepper."

"Hello, Tony?" He heard her cheery voice from the distant planet below.

"Pepper! Wanna go to a restaurant on the moon?"

"Why would we do that, Tony? There's no atmosphere! Let me guess....you're in space?"

"How'd you know? I just made some changes to the Zipsat. We can IM each other now without phone companies."

"Is it secure? I have some updates to send you on Kinshasa. I'm at the airport now, heading to Kabul. Wait one minute, I have to go through passport control."

Tony heard some shuffling on the other end as Pepper put down her phone and spoke French to a distant border officer. He checked the Zipsat one last time and unhooked his safety harness from the satellite, letting the retractable cables wind back into his armor. Then he set a course for the rendezvous point.

Iron Man rocketed down toward Earth, at first by following the coordinates, then by sight once he spotted the space plane, its wings pivoted up. Tavares X-2 used rockets to ascend, but its wings rotated up on hinges once the plane was in the upper atmosphere. They'd pivot back into place for a traditional runway landing after the plane descended to fifteen miles above the Earth.

"Jarvis, take a few photos, will you? That's a fine piece of engineering. Send one to Geoff and the board, with a note: 'Wish you were here.'"

He heard Pepper now, arguing with someone at the airport.

"Those are not priceless antiques, and I do not owe a fine! That was carved yesterday in front of me in a small village. You just want a bribe. You should be ashamed of yourself."

He cruised down toward the space plane. Bored, he tried looking for man-made objects on the Earth's surface—but even with enhanced optics, he saw nothing but a swirl of blue ocean, brown and green continents, and white clouds. "Jarvis, send note to National Geographic. Stark: Confirm, no sighting of Great Wall from space."

"Tony, still there?"

"Hey, Pepper. That sounded like fun. Do you know why the cow went to outer space?"

"To jump over the moon?"

"No. To visit the Milky Way."

She laughed a little. She sounded tired after her discussion with Congolese airport authorities.

"Pepper, I'm flying to meet a space plane, and, you know, I'm looking at Earth, and the view is amazing. It never gets old. And it makes you feel so small and insignificant. Life goes so quickly." He had a spontaneous urge to tell Pepper his true feelings for her. "Pepper, there's something I've been meaning to tell you—"

She cut him off. "Tony, are you wearing space pants?"

"What? Why?"

"Because your ass is out of this world. Gotta go, we're taking off. I'll call you when you're back on terra firma."

The line went dead, just as Tony approached Tavares X-2. It was already descending, its nose pointed down toward the Earth far, far below.

"Iron Man on approach. Hudson, do you copy?"

"Hudson here. We copy, Stark, but we're getting unusual instrument readings. Lotta malfunction potential here. Sorry, Iron Man. We wanted to do you a favor, but it looks like we might need *your* help instead. Can you eyeball our wings? Something's wrong up there."

"No problem. I owe you one. You guys saved me a lot of time and fuel by giving me a lift."

Iron Man fired up his boot jets and sped closer to the space plane. He circled around it twice and noticed a dark spot near the wing.

"Hudson, I'm flying in and latching myself to your starboard side. Don't be alarmed. I'm taking a closer look."

He zoomed in close now, glad for his armor's precise navigation system. Iron Man paced himself alongside the plane, then reeled out his retractable cables and latched on to two adjacent steel eyelets.

"Record mission: Tavares X-2 repair in motion. Location: Earth's mesosphere. Datestamp. Ohh, wait. *Urgh,*" said Tony. "Motion sickness. I feel like I want to throw up. Definitely prefer flying under my own power.

"Attached to space plane. Shooting video now of damage near wing. Jarvis, Zipsat photos to Galaxy FLX. Request repair information."

Tony knew he didn't have long to sort this problem out. They'd reenter the stratosphere in a few minutes, and the wings had to be down then if the plane had any hope of making a safe landing. Or any landing. Without wings to slow down the reentry, the only way this plane wouldn't burn up would be if Iron Man himself carried it the last 70,000 feet.

Fixing the problem here, in the outer atmosphere, would sure be a lot easier.

"Jarvis: Send reminder to me when I'm back at Coney Island. Research variables of Iron Man Mark II space armor carrying a hybrid rocket space plane safely to Earth.

"Hudson," Tony continued, "the good news is it's not your wings. They're ready to pivot into place for a glide landing."

"And the bad news?"

"You've got a hole back here where something fell off. Do your instruments indicate what might have been under this panel?"

"Stability is fluctuating."

Galaxy FLX Mission Control, back on Earth, cut

in now. "Hudson, according to that photo Stark just sent, you've got a missing gyroscopic navigational sensor. We need a new gyroscope, or else Iron Man's gonna have to carry you in."

"Negative, HQ," said Tony. "Carrying this plane home is worst-case scenario. The Mark II armor works great up here, but once we get into the atmosphere, gravity turns it into rock stockings."

"Any ideas?" asked the voice from HQ. "We like our plane, Mister Stark. We'd like to bring it home in one piece."

Hudson interrupted. "Don't forget me. I know this plane costs more than a pilot, but I've got to pick up milk for my wife on the way home."

"Affirmative, Hudson. Pilots are expensive to replace, too."

"Stand by," said Tony. He studied the connectors, then sighed.

"I'm not real fond of this idea, but it's the best I've got," he said. "Jarvis, confirm solvency of extravehicular mobility gyroscopic-navigational compartment. I'm going to open it, but it's got to be quarantined from my primary life-support subsystem."

"Extravehicular mobility compartment is sealed."

"All right, open it and extend the robotic clip wire." Mark II was bulky, and Tony always had a hard time with the oversized gloves on the armor. *This has to be how the Hulk feels,* he thought. *Or maybe Ben Grimm.* Clumsily, he grabbed the clip and jammed it into the space plane's empty equipment bay. His gloves blocked his view, giving him only brief glimpses inside the compartment now.

Tony randomly moved the clip around until he saw a spark. That was it. He latched the clip on, hardwiring the Mark II armor's navigational system into the plane. Now Iron Man *was* the plane's navigational system.

"Hudson, you're good to about 13,000 feet, but I've got to cut off of this once your wings go down or I'll compromise your flight."

"Then what?"

"I'm still working that part out." He turned back to the job at hand. "Jarvis, fine-focus. Give me a laser. I'm cutting out Mark II's navigational gyroscope."

"Proceeding through space without the ability to navigate is not recommended."

"Yeah, Jarvis, I know," said Tony. "We're going to ride this plane to 13,000 feet, then cut loose just before the wings go down. We still have an emergency chute, right? Let me know when we're over Texas. I'll use thruster micro-bursts to adjust my fall and send us in the right direction."

Iron Man focused on the job at hand, lasering components from the Mark II while carefully avoiding compromising life support and thrusters. By working intently, he found he could almost ignore his slight motion sickness.

He used a robotic-arm grip to firmly position the components inside the space plane. *Don't need anything slipping and floating away up here,* he thought.

"Jarvis, send photo to Galactic FLX Mission Control."

He heard a response a moment later. Zipsat sure was fast.

"Nice work, Iron Man. We have tiles on the wings, but these are just a precaution. Our high-drag descent eliminates need for these except in an emergency. Pry off a tile and you should be able to form a new seal with it. How exactly are you getting down without any stabilizers?"

"With a headache and a side of nausea," said Tony. "Jarvis, inject Dramamine and prepare for release. Set the automatic activation device to open the chute if I pass out or exceed 35 meters a second. Hudson, have a good flight. You're on your own now."

Iron Man unclipped his retractable cables and heard a sharp snap as they zipped back into his armor. Tavares X-2 tore away from him, beginning its descent to the Texas runway. Tony marveled as its wings unfolded incrementally, pivoting slowly until they were in place for a runway landing as on a typical airplane.

Marvelous, he thought. *Brilliant design, like a badminton shuttlecock. May have to modify the Avengers Quinjet like that.*

But as much as he wanted to watch the space plane's landing, Tony had his own rudderless flight to worry about.

"Mini-propulsion thrusts," said Tony. He descended slowly for a few feet, first using his right repulsor, then his left.

"Jarvis, automate parachute deployment in—*whoa!*"

Suddenly off-balance, Tony lurched unexpectedly.

"No, no, gimme a boost, even on both…" He spun now, in sickening spirals.

"Jets, now!" Tony yelled. His boot jets fired; he regained control momentarily, then began spinning again—but head-over-heels this time, and a lot faster.

"I'm gonna need more Dramamine," he muttered. "Jarvis, automate makeshift stability calculations and run the thrusters." He slowed down, but didn't stop completely. Iron Man lurched from side to side as Jarvis tried to steady him with mini-bursts.

"Let's try this again. Power into neutral and just use the chute. An old-fashioned skydive."

"Thrusters are offline."

Iron Man went into freefall and wished for a moment that he could feel the wind rush past his cheeks—but the Mark II was necessarily airtight, and getting more clunky and uncomfortable now that he was only ten miles from the ground.

"Drogue, NOW!"

The pilot chute fluttered up and caught the wind, inflating, creating drag that slowed Iron Man's fall. Tony felt himself stabilize as he fell, the sound of air rushing past him. The main chute unfolded next, opening slowly as the slider worked its way down the canopy.

And then Tony was gliding peacefully over Texas.

"Jarvis, cut the white noise. Cut all noise. Turn off

everything but life support. I want to hear nothing but the wind in the chute."

Iron Man descended a few miles in near-silence. He gazed around him. Finally his phone rang.

"Answer."

"Tony, it's Maya. Are you okay? You're running later than you said you would."

"Sorry, Maya. I had a few things to take care of on the way. I'm near..." He glanced at the GPS readout on his HUD. "Waco. My driver is heading up to get me. We won't be long. Still up for that late lunch?"

"Maybe. I'm not hungry. I feel nauseous."

"That makes two of us. Give it some time. Maybe we'll be hungry later. See you soon."

He clicked off and silenced all incoming communications. Then he smiled.

Tony Stark was a mile up in the sky, descending with the help of wind and gravity. He didn't want to hear about Maya's problems or Stark Enterprises' latest dilemma.

He just wanted to admire the view.

SEVEN

Tony tested more of his new Zipsat functionality by beaming a text to Maya from the Austin airport. It worked: She was waiting outside Futurepharm when the sleek, black Stark sedan pulled up at the suburban office park.

Maya's head was bowed and her arms were crossed over a pink silk blouse. Her hair, much longer than it used to be, was pulled back in a simple ponytail. She was older now, but still stunning.

"Maya..." said Tony as he stepped out of the back seat. She moved toward him, and then she was in his arms.

"Whoa, whoa." He was surprised by this show of emotion. Last time he'd seen Maya, she'd been so engrossed in her job, she hadn't noticed when he'd flirted with both the restaurant hostess and the waitress. She'd been too busy jotting down formulas on a napkin.

Now she was crying.

"What's wrong?" He held her close. Her hair smelled like apples. *Remember Mrs. Rennie's advice,* thought Tony. He thought of Pepper, en route to Kabul, and altered his assessment. Maya's hair smelled like apple shampoo that might have needed a bit more rinsing.

"There was a bang, Tony," said Maya once she could talk over her tears. "I rushed into Al's office to see what happened. Al was...part of his head was missing. I called the paramedics, but..."

"Ouch. Too late?" *Oops,* thought Tony. *Easy on the humor here.* Or would it help take her mind off the situation?

"And he'd left a note on the printer. His, I don't know, confession. Al—Dr. Killian, my project director—stole the Extremis dose. Gave it away to someone. We don't know who."

"What's Extremis?"

"My project." Maya pulled back.

She had a desperate look about her. Something was seriously wrong—even more wrong than a dead project director.

"Calm down. Let's go in and take a look at Killian's office. What were you wearing when you found him?"

"My lab coat. Why?"

"I just like to know what you were wearing." *That should do it,* he thought.

She smiled slightly. "Still a hit with the ladies, I see. You haven't changed, Tony. Though you did grow some facial hair."

"Plus, I'm a super hero now, and...actually, I've stopped chasing women."

"What?" Maya quickly glanced at his ring finger. "Impossible. No way has Tony Stark settled down."

"Not exactly," Tony admitted. "I've stopped chasing women, *mostly*. Except this one who...uh, she knows I'm alive, but not like that. I'm still working on her seeing me as more than a pest who sends her on classified missions and pays for her new passport every few years."

"I see." Tony thought he detected a hint of iciness in Maya's reaction. Was she jealous? "Is that the Mrs. Rennie I spoke to?"

"What? Good lord, no. Mrs. Rennie is my secretary and trainer. She trains me to get out of bed and attend meetings. Plus, she's, like, a hundred."

"I read in the *World-Star* that Tony Stark likes older women."

"I don't like any women! No, I mean, I do, I like women just fine. Some of my best friends are women... just not like that. Not like in the *World-Star*. I'm a one-woman man now, Maya. Or I will be, if I can just convince the one woman that I'm not the playboy she's known for more than a decade."

He stopped now, noticing that Maya had raised one eyebrow slightly and was viewing him with skepticism. "People don't change," she said. "The Tony Stark I knew would pick up the waitress while his date pretended not to notice by scribbling formulas on napkins."

"Oh. You caught that. Well, hey, all in the past now. What I was trying to tell you is I don't drink anymore, and I don't make guns anymore. See, people *do* change. Stark is going to make phones and heaters and battery-powered toenail clippers…and maybe even some robot vacuum cleaners. The same stuff I was making fun of back when we first met at Techwest."

She pulled back, surprised. "But you said…"

"I know what I said. I can't claim I was young and stupid, because I've never been stupid. But I've learned a lot about taking the moral way forward, and I accept responsibility for my actions now. Come on, take me inside. I want to help you."

Tony led her into the building by the hand, then pushed open the heavy door to Killian's office.

"The computer's still here?" Tony was surprised. He studied the hardware in front of him for a moment.

"The police have been and gone. They said they're sending another team to pick it up. We can't break its security."

Tony pulled his phone out of his pocket and glanced at it. He pecked away at on-screen icons while Maya waited.

"Hm. The Extremis project—was it your field?" Tony spoke absentmindedly.

"Bioelectrics. Robotic microsurgery," said Maya.

Tony pushed a button on the phone, pressed a few keys, then held the Stark Beam 01 up to his ear.

"Markko? Tony Stark. I need a favor, much more your area of expertise than consumer appliances. You're about to receive an entire encrypted hard drive via Zipsat. It's uploading now. I need it cracked, then upload the raw data to my secure private server. Okay? Stand by. And Markko? Nice touch adding the screaming to the Stark space heater."

Tony clicked off the call, but continued holding the phone out so that he could watch the progress bar.

"Zipsat?" Now it was Maya's turn to ask questions.

"My own constellation of satellites providing wireless broadband, independent of telecom networks. And of course, *much* faster."

"You're streaming an entire hard drive?" She shifted uncomfortably. "What else can that phone do?"

"Every episode of *Billionaire Boys and Their Toys* is on here. Wanna watch?"

"Sounds dreadful."

"Fascinating show if plasma-fired shape-shifting touchscreens are your cup of tea."

"You know, the *World-Star* calls you a ladies' man, but I can't imagine this sort of chitchat does more than make women's eyes glaze over."

"Being one of the wealthiest men on earth usually does the trick. But why are you reading that rag? You're not exactly its target audience. Have I mentioned I'm suing them?" Tony's phone emitted a beep. "There, done."

"I just see the headlines at the supermarket checkout," said Maya sheepishly.

"I know it's late, Maya, but let's go out for lunch. You've had a rough couple of days. What's around here? We're pretty far from town."

"There's a breakfast taco place that's open all day."

"I have a better idea. There's a winery that serves meals. It's in Sonoma. We could drop in on Sal."

"You think?" Maya had her arms crossed and was glaring at Tony now. Either she thought he was being totally unrealistic, or she *really* wanted breakfast tacos.

"He's still in the Bay Area, right? Sal's your friend. My friend. And he knows a lot about your field and my field. And let's face it, this office is a downer right now."

"I don't know. I don't feel like packing at the moment, and the police might have more questions. Plus, that sounds ridiculous."

"Packing, hell," said Tony. "My plane's on standby, and my car comes with it. I have a very fast plane. You'll be back here for dinner. Let's get out of here for a while."

"How fast is this plane?"

"Similar to the Quinjet design I gave to the Avengers. Only—you know—faster. Better robots. And a giant Stark logo on the side."

Maya smiled that familiar old quirky smile. "You are so weird." She poked Tony in the chest.

"Hey, easy on the heart," he said, play-slapping her hand away.

Tony Zipsat-beamed Happy to bring the car back around.

......

"**W**e should've borrowed my cousin's license plates this morning." Beck slumped back in the passenger seat of the gray Econoline.

"I got a screwdriver. Maybe we can swipe a couple when we stop for gas," said Nilsen, glancing at the dashboard gauges. "There's enough in the tank to make it to highway 10, but I'll have to stop before Houston."

"So long as we don't have to pull over in one of these podunk small towns where everyone knows each other and the sheriff sees exactly who drives in and out every day. Should've filled up before we left Bastrop. We know exactly where the cops hang out there." Beck glanced accusingly back at Mallen.

"Where we get gas doesn't matter anymore," growled Mallen from the back seat. "The law's got no right to control what we do with this van. It's Nilsen's. Where he drives is none of their business."

"I know that, and you know that, but I don't think they know that." Beck chuckled. "And I'm not supposed to leave the county. I'm still on probation for that phone call to my ex."

"You idiot," said Mallen. "She was only out of jail ten minutes before she was back on the meth. You could've just avoided her. They locked her up again fast enough."

"Her stupidity is why the kids got taken away. I never would've gone after her if she wasn't a worthless addict, making up all that crap about me fighting dogs and shoplifting ladders at the hardware store. Why the hell would I fight dogs? Dogs are good for hunting and guarding the house. If I want a fight, I'll go find one myself."

"Where'd they put the kids?"

"Her sister has them in Austin. Won't let me see them. They're in public school, probably eating tofu and learning Spanish, and getting taught all kinds of crap. I heard they let you burn flags now."

"We'll go get your kids after this, Beck. Kids oughta be with their father. The law can't tell you not to see your kids."

"You seem awful sure of yourself, Mallen." Nilsen's eyes met Mallen's through the rearview mirror. Nilsen was normally the leader of this dysfunctional trio, but he'd been demoted to second-in-command when Mallen had lurched out of the slaughterhouse yesterday.

Mallen didn't care whether Nilsen was questioning his authority. He was thinking about what came after Houston.

"Nobody's gonna bother us anymore. No one's going to bother any real Americans anymore."

"Don't mess with Mallen." Nilsen snickered.

"Did you feel that?" Mallen was suddenly on alert.

Beck and Nilsen glanced at each other. They'd obviously felt nothing. Mallen realized they thought he was cracking up, but a minute later they heard the thumping, too.

"Just a flat," said Nilsen, steering the van to the side of the road.

Nilsen and Beck got out of the van and went

around to the rear to look for the spare. Mallen slid open the side door and took a look at the flat tire.

"You ran over glass. Man, look where you're going next time."

Nilsen rolled the spare out of the van. He pushed it over next to the flat tire, pried off the hubcap, and got to work loosening the lug nuts.

"Where's your jack?" Beck climbed into the van to dig around. "Whoa!" Mallen heard Beck tumble, hitting the back of the passenger seat as the van suddenly jolted.

Mallen had reached down and lifted up the rear of the van with two hands. He stood holding it, bored. He wasn't straining his arms at all.

"Y'all don't need a jack," he said.

"Don't let go, man." Nilsen hurriedly pulled off the flat tire and replaced it with the spare. He finished quickly, and Mallen lowered the Econoline back to the pavement.

Beck climbed out of the van and slid down the bumper on to the gravel along the shoulder of the highway. Nilsen let the old tire spiral down to the ground with a thud. Then they both stood and stared at Mallen.

"Daaaang, Mallen. You might actually be useful now," said Nilsen. He let out a low whistle.

"So yeah, I guess it doesn't matter where we get gas," said Beck. "Hell, let's not even pay sales tax."

"Let's get a move on to Houston," said Mallen. "There's some people I wanna see at the FBI."

EIGHT

"He's off on his wild-man-in-the-woods kick again, isn't he?" said Maya, standing next to Tony at the end of a two-mile dirt road near Occidental in California's Sonoma County.

"I like it better than his minimalist raw-foodist phase."

Tony pushed ahead through some tall grass to get to Sal's front door. The house looked spacious, new, and mostly conventional aside from a particleboard addition covered only in Tyvek.

"Sitting in a room with no furniture getting your lungs seared out by his farts? No, thanks," said Maya. She motioned at a bathtub sitting outside to the right of the front door. "Look, at least he's got plumbing."

"Of a sort," said Tony, pointing up to a rainwatercollection tank on the roof. "Running water supplied by rain and gravity."

She shuddered. "I need a drink, but not here. I don't want to be forced to inspect the toilet facilities."

Tony stepped up on to the porch and pushed the doorbell. He heard a distant melody, then tilted his head.

"What music is that doorbell playing?"

"Something by the Grateful Dead, I think." Maya crossed her arms over her pink silk blouse and pursed her lips.

"Who?"

"Come on, Tony. Don't pretend you don't know what I'm talking about."

Tony smirked.

Sal opened the door. "My children," he said, spreading his arms wide. "Come in, come in. Welcome to utopia! You want I should twist up a bomber?"

Tony eyed Sal with his garish flower-print short-sleeve shirt, tinted glasses, shaggy white hair and beard, and old iPod slung around his neck on a string. "Not me," Tony said. "I swore off that stuff. And I might have to fly later."

"I don't touch it anymore, either," claimed Maya. Sal skeptically raised his eyebrows. "Makes me…uh… sleepy."

Sal feigned shock as he led his visitors in past a hall-way of carved West African masks and his own impressionistic landscape paintings. "My children have become weenie straight people! The horror. Well, come on through. I just pressed some apple juice."

They reached the living room. The walls were almost all glass and faced west to catch the afternoon sun. Sal motioned them to two wooden chairs around a table. "Sit, sit," he said. "I know it doesn't look like much to you military/industrial-funded types, but it suits me now."

"I'm solo, Sal," said Tony. "And Maya's salaried by an independent—"

"Yes, yes," said Sal impatiently. "Military. Corporations. Government. S.H.I.E.L.D. Hair-splitting. You fail to see they are all the same thing. These are inescapable truths. You cannot do the science without stepping into their filthy pool." He poured three glasses of juice from a carafe and passed them out. Maya sipped hers cautiously.

"I do a whole rap about this at a learning colony at Big Sur in the summertime, you know. Under the teaching tree."

"The teaching tree." Maya raised her eyebrows while Tony rolled his eyes.

"Yeah, I know." Sal laughed and sat down in his easy chair. He raised his glass. "Tech people go out there, too. There's one guy who believes all technological innovation should be done *from the heart*. He takes his code monkeys out there and makes them do yoga 'til they puke." He chortled gleefully. *"It gets the heart center working."*

Tony just stared. Sal was brilliant, but he took some patience.

"This is the problem with thinking at this level. The basic truths—that America is now being run as a post-political corporate conglomerate—are too bitter to swallow. It is easier for half-smart people to think the path to freedom requires you to stand on one leg for an hour."

Maya frowned. "I do yoga, Sal. It calms me down when I'm angry."

"You used to use Jack Daniels for that."

"Still do, sometimes, but it makes it hard to get my job done."

"We're facing up to the future," continued Sal. "But we can't see it. I always thought it'd be you two who'd be road-testing the future for us. But you, Maya, you're stuck essentially punching biological structure until it gives up and does what you want." He pointed at her accusingly.

"And Tony, you've fiddled with some medical patents and built weapons, and now you've made a superhero suit."

Tony tried the juice and spat it back out. *Gross.*

"She's the Edward Teller of biology, and you're the Dean Kamen of technology."

Tony firmly placed his glass down on the table. "That's not fair," he said. "Dean Kamen's done good, useful work."

"Yeah, but what's he known for? The Segway. And Clive Sinclair? He made Britain a center of excellence for consumer microcomputing, but all he's remembered for is the C5, which was a Segway with pedals. Tony Stark will be remembered for working out how to sneeze inside a mask.

"You two are going to your graves with the epitaphs *'Almost Useful.'"*

Sal glared at his two juniors, then cracked a smile. "But then, so am I." He leaned his head back and laughed, his belly rocking.

Tony shook his head, hoping Sal was wrong about him. He'd done a lot more than invent gadgets. He wished he didn't have to wonder whether he might be more a combination of Kamen and Teller, the father of the hydrogen bomb. His earlier conversation with Bellingham still haunted him.

Mallen, now dressed in a hip-length leather coat and brown T-shirt over jeans, kicked open the van's rear doors from the inside and leapt to the pavement.

"Wait here," he growled at Nilsen.

"Right here? In front of FBI headquarters?"

In response, Mallen just bared his teeth and grinned before heading past the gate to the green building's main entrance. Nilsen shrugged and looked quizzically at Beck, but he stayed parked. Mallen was about to prove himself to his friends.

And to everyone else, too.

Back in Occidental, Tony decided to change the subject. "What are you working on right now?"

"Mostly," said Sal, raising his eyebrows, "I'm taking drugs. I spend my days cooking down Illinois bundleweed into DMT and raising mushrooms."

Tony sighed with exasperation. "You and your damn psychedelics." He picked up one of the books on the coffee table and read the back-cover copy about Aldous Huxley's adventures taking mescaline.

"You never would drop LSD, would you?"

"I left that to the computer geniuses. Anyway, I liked whisky better. I'm in recovery now—from lots of things, actually. Now I drink water."

"Good for you," said Sal. "I've come to consider LSD as abrasively psychiatric. It really just reruns all your memory stores at random. DMT and mushrooms are much more interesting and alive."

Tony exchanged a glance with Maya. Sometimes Sal could be visionary. Other times, he seemed in need of intervention. DMT was a natural hallucinogen that, some people believed, could access hidden parts of the brain. Historically, it had been used by shamans in South America and hadn't been studied much. Except, apparently, by Sal.

Sal continued. "DMT interests me because it gets you to a place beyond your memory stores. You know something like sixty percent of people have the same hallucinations on DMT? Terence McKenna, rest his soul, called them 'self-transforming machine elves.' Little technological artifacts that spoke a basic machine code that, no matter what your language, you could understand."

Maya was listening intently now. She'd been rewiring the brain using science. What Sal was describing had the same effect, but his technique involved psychiatric substances instead of revisions of physical code. Tony wondered for a minute whether all three of them had the same aim—of accessing and revising human power—but different techniques.

"McKenna thought he'd accessed the afterlife. *I* think it's the operating system of the human body."

That was it, then: Sal was working on the same biological brain design that Maya had been working on. Tony looked at Maya and wondered whether she realized this. Sal almost certainly had, but he was goading his protégés now, pushing an agenda on them without stating where he was going.

"The brain is actually designed to take in and process DMT. Did you know that? I think we're *supposed* to take it. Supposed to see our own operating systems. And perhaps we're supposed to hack them. Perhaps we're supposed to change our own bodies."

Tony was still skeptical. He did not reply.

"Drugs are technologies, Tony," said Sal, as if he were lecturing a small, uninformed child. "In the places where humanity first arose, there were psychedelic mushrooms. It's a medical fact that those mushrooms improve visual acuity. That would make early humans better hunters. The Iron Man suit you built, Tony—it has sensors, zoom lenses, and the like?"

"Yes." Tony leaned forward. Maybe this was going somewhere relevant, after all.

Maya still hadn't moved. She already could see what Sal's rantings had to do with her research.

"Same thing. So you can see better. So could early humans who had mushrooms in their diet. Maya, your Extremis process—it redesigns the human eye, too?"

"Yeah. And other senses."

"And you were both in the business of making better hunters. Haven't strayed far from the pack, have you? Why are you here?"

Tony looked at Maya. "Advice."

"Ah," said Sal. "Come to see the wise man of the forest. The old shaman. You know what they call a shaman in Australia? The clever fella. So which one of you is in trouble?"

Maya glanced away. "That would be me."

"Let me guess. The super-soldier thing. Your old obsession. Microelectronic plug-ins for the brain?"

"Yeah."

Sal sighed and continued. "No one else has ever gotten a result like old Erskine did with Captain America."

Tony listened intently. Captain America was a friend and colleague. His peak-human abilities didn't require technology and armor, as Iron Man's did. Cap's internal biological structure had been altered more than seventy years ago by a process that had never been replicated. Maya's research had come closest.

Sal was still talking. He talked a lot. "You know what a Hieronymus Machine is?"

"Yeah," said Tony. "It's junk in a box. Pseudoscience that does nothing."

"Wrong," said Sal. "It works exactly to the experimenter's intent. It's a mock-up that channels willpower. Some people think Erskine's Super-Soldier Serum was a Hieronymus Machine—that it was simply his own force of will that made it work exactly like a perfect super-soldier dose."

"That's ridiculous," said Tony. "You're discounting the determination of Steve Rogers. Plus, if willpower created science, ambitious villains all over the world would be super-powered."

Sal jabbed a finger at Tony angrily. "You're both in trouble. It's just that *you* don't know it yet."

Stunned, Tony went silent. He'd expected this visit to Sal's would be about Maya, not himself.

"You can barely look at yourself in the mirror anymore. Right, Tony? You're rich, independent of the military. I have a feeling you do good works when you can. But it's not enough. Your intellect and power isn't enough for you. There's a dam across your life. Built of guilt and locked in place. You want to move forward, but you can't."

Now Sal pointed at Maya. "Her problem is she's a woman. There's a glass ceiling. It could take her years to get to where you are now—longer, since she's dependent on other people's money. And what would you do, Maya, if you got to Tony's position?"

"Four years of devoted engineering, and I could cure cancer." Maya looked determined, dead-set on her goal. If willpower really could create a serum, she looked to be the one to do it.

"There you go," said Sal. "And what do you think of at night, Tony?"

"Making a better Iron Man suit."

"So you can wrestle monsters or whatever it is you do?"

Enough, thought Tony. Sal had gone too far. "No. And your juice stinks."

"So what does Iron Man do aside from beating up Fin Fang Foom?"

"Stark Enterprises was complicit in war. Iron Man is going to stop it."

Sal laughed gently at Tony's noble intentions. "It'd be hard to kill someone wearing an Iron Man suit," said Sal. "For a year. Until the suit's specs were superseded. If they haven't been already."

He pointed at Maya, who looked away. "Perhaps by her. Or perhaps by her work's tendency toward emergent behavior. Think about it, Tony. Captain America doesn't need a suit. Won't *someone* eventually come along who's bigger and stronger? And he might not be trying to help people."

"Cap's not better than me," grumbled Tony.

"Don't change the subject, Tony. Is a suit really the best you can do? Maya's working on military apps because that's how she's going to get the funding to cure disease. What about you?

"What's the Iron Man *for,* Tony?"

Tony did not respond.

Mallen approached the security checkpoint in the FBI lobby. His appearance was unassuming and utterly average for a Texan in his mid-30s, and the strange alien cocoon he'd grown back in the slaughterhouse had sloughed off completely. His short brown hair was starting to recede on his forehead even as new wrinkles had begun to form. He bore an intense look of concentration, and a furrowed brow.

He could have taken off his coat and passed it through the X-ray machine, as the half-dozen visitors ahead of him just had. He could have simply walked through the metal detector. He wasn't even carrying house keys or coins. And he no longer needed weapons.

He was a weapon.

Mallen looked up at the surveillance camera, challenged it with a sneer, then glared at the security guard next to the X-ray machine.

"Your coat, sir," said the guard, firmly and politely.

Mallen responded with a fierce right cross, a punch so strong it smashed the man's face, splattering blood and teeth across the tile floor. As the guard collapsed, Mallen tore away the man's gun holster.

A second guard came at Mallen now. He wore a ballistics vest as all the lobby guards did. But Mallen had no intention of firing the gun he'd just acquired.

He pulled the handgun from its holster and threw it at the second guard.

The gun hit the man squarely in the chest with the impact of a cannonball. He flew back, knocking over the retractable belt barrier, and landed on the floor. Mallen didn't hesitate. He headed straight to the fallen guard and gutted him with a single swipe. Mallen's fingers were like talons, slicing straight through flesh as if it were slow-cooked brisket.

Three other guards aimed guns at Mallen now. He saw businesspeople and visitors running from the lobby.

He looked at his bloodied hands and the two dead men in front of him with surprise. The injection had made Mallen far more powerful than he'd dreamed of becoming.

He cracked his knuckles and ferociously launched himself at the remaining guards as they fired their weapons.

The bullets tore through Mallen's jacket and shirt, but all they did was leave slight, temporary dents in his face. Mallen ripped one man right in half and pulped the other's head with his hand. The final security guard fired point-blank at Mallen, who broke the man's neck with a swing of his fist.

Civilians and federal employees all scrambled to escape the lobby, but Mallen stood between them and the entrance. A man in a business suit frantically stabbed at the elevator "Up" button. The only way out was behind those sliding doors.

Mallen felt an unfamiliar tickle in his throat. *Dang,* he thought, as he realized what it was. He inhaled deeply, his breath collecting as a blue mist.

He forced out a plume of orange flame, expelling deeply with his stomach muscles.

A half-dozen men in ties and jackets were vaporized in Mallen's path, leaving behind only crumbling piles of ash and DNA. Others flailed, on fire, howling unholy screams until their lungs collapsed and they fell to the floor. Mallen incinerated them with another blazing outburst. People who had rushed away from their families this morning, grocery lists in hand, boxed lunches left uneaten, were all reduced to spots of smoldering fire.

Two men had been crouching just outside Mallen's range. "Oops, missed you," he said. He grabbed one man's face with his left hand and squeezed, then impaled the other on his right fist.

The elevator door still hadn't opened, so Mallen forced it ajar. He breathed plumes of fire into the chute, circulating flames up to other floors, then reached up and tore the electrical panel out of the shaft wall. No one would escape this way.

Mallen took a deep breath, waited for the hot kindling tickle in his throat, then shot out enough fire to ignite the entire lobby. Satisfied now, he stood and watched as black smoke rose from unmoving shapes, as briefcases and bagged lunches smoldered.

"Smells like a barbeque," he said. He'd torched the entire ground level. He looked around once more: The FBI building was a fiery inferno.

Mallen calmly left the building, an eerie silhouette walking unharmed among the flames.

Sal had made his point to Tony, gotten him thinking. Now Sal sat back and relaxed a bit. "I tried to inculcate in both of you a sense of the future," he said. "As far back as Techwest. Remember that? You turned up drunk, and he turned up in a suit.

"But you both had the future in you. Why aren't you already running the table?"

Tony was silent now, and so was Maya, but then a buzzing broke the silence.

"Sorry," said Maya, reaching into her front pocket. "Phone."

She listened to someone in Austin talk for a minute, then spoke. "Sal, can you put on CNN?"

"I don't have a TV or an Internet connection."

Tony interrupted. "I'll stream it from my phone to your laptop. I assume that thing is charged?"

"Uh, no," said Sal, a bit sheepishly. He pushed a button on a remote and a diesel generator started up outside the living room window.

"Sal. Fossil fuels?" Now it was Tony's turn to smirk.

"We're all ethically compromised." Sal shrugged. "You fly that plane of yours all over. I keep my beer cold. My lights run on solar, and wind turbines power my lab, but my beer refrigerator and laptop run on rotten dinosaurs."

As Tony streamed the news from his phone to the laptop, the three of them watched Mallen's unfolding horror show in Houston. The FBI building was on fire, and burning corpses could be seen within the lobby. A banner across the bottom of the screen warned viewers that graphic images were being displayed.

"Yeah, I'm here." Maya was still on the phone with Futurepharm. "Tony, can you turn up the sound?"

The volume bars on the laptop monitor lit up as Tony pushed a slider on his phone screen. A live newscaster with a microphone was standing outside the building.

"...few survivors we spoke to indicate an un-armed man did all this, disabling the elevators and torching the ground level, trapping the building's staff in a rising blaze and leaving the living and the dead to be incinerated in the lobby. Almost surreal scenes of—oh, God, move the camera. I'm sorry..."

A firefighter in a respirator looked up at the camera. He was lifting the head of a deeply burned victim, still breathing but scarred and half-covered in bandages. The victim's lips had been disintegrated, leaving his or her—it was impossible to tell—teeth exposed to the camera. An EMT glanced at the camera as it swung away from the victim.

Now the newscaster was interviewing an eyewitness, a burned man.

"He was...he was breathing fire. You could see the ripple of gas coming out of his throat— and, and then he came back, and things came out of his hands..."

The witness broke down into sobs. Tony turned the stream off. "Why are we watching this, Maya?"

"The signatures." She wouldn't meet his eyes. "The fire. The hands. A few other things. An Extremis enhancile did this."

Maya closed her eyes and looked terribly pained. "Whoever stole the Extremis dose took it, Tony. And lived, and did this. But the anger—"

"Maybe he should have tried yoga," Sal interrupted.

She opened her eyes, shocked by his inappropriate humor, but then Sal came over and put an arm around his protégé. He took her hand.

Tony picked up his phone again. "Happy, we're coming back. Get the plane prepped for immediate return to Austin. And have Mrs. Rennie inform the authorities that Iron Man will assist the investigation of the incident at the Houston FBI."

Mallen crouched in the back of Nilsen's van as the three men drove along Interstate 10, heading east out of Houston. No one worried about license plates anymore. All the authorities were preoccupied with the fiery nightmare at the FBI building, and not likely to notice a single vehicle pulling away from downtown.

Beck and Nilsen had been silent ever since Mallen had leapt back through the Econoline's rear double-doors, lit by the dancing orange flames licking up along the sides of the FBI headquarters. Now, as Nilsen drove, Beck finally swung an arm over the passenger seat and leaned back to face Mallen, who saw fear in his friend's eyes. *Good,* he thought.

"What did you do, Mallen?"

"What did I do?" Mallen's sneer con torted with a mixture of delight and fury.

"I just *started.*"

NINE

Tony's first full day outside the garage in weeks had been complicated. He sat aboard the Stark Enterprises jet, staring at Maya, who held herself stiffly in the cushioned seat directly across from him. The sun was setting as they flew from the Bay Area back to Austin, producing brilliant hues of orange and pink that doused the passenger compartment in kaleidoscopic light.

"I'd almost forgotten what a sunset looked like," Tony mused. "I was shut up in my workshop on Coney Island for a month and a half."

Maya was obviously too miserable to enjoy the sunset. She stared into space.

"Hey, Maya, remember me? Tony Stark? You called me, asked me to come talk to you? Was that a literal request? Because I'm talking plenty and you, you're not talking much at all."

She said nothing.

"I could've gone to a fun meeting today, you know. At least they'd have talked back to me. The board has *lots* to say. Won't shut up, in fact."

"My project," she whispered finally. "Used as a weapon."

"How can you be sure?" Tony asked.

"Aside from the clear signatures and the computer analysis on the video news report that my staff performed? It happened within driving distance of Futurepharm. Inside of a couple of days of a successful Extremis installation time period."

"Extremis." Tony turned the word over in his head a few times. "I think it's time you told me all about Extremis." He put his elbows on to the table, interlocked his fingers, and leaned his chin forward on to his hands.

Maya closed her eyes before answering. Her greatest invention had possibly just slaughtered fifty people. *This must be hard for her*, Tony realized.

"Have you got anything to drink?"

"Sal gave me some of his apple juice to take back to Mrs. Rennie."

"Gross. No. That's not what I had in mind." She opened her eyes, but didn't look at Tony. He kept his gaze steady and fierce.

"Extremis is a super-soldier solution," she continued. "It's a bio-electronics package. Fitted into a few billion graphic nanotubes and suspended in a carrier fluid.

A magic bullet. Like the original Super-Soldier Serum, all in a single injection."

"So it's what Sal suggested," said Tony. "Exactly what he said. What you've been working on your entire adult life. Longer than I've known you. It hacks the body."

Maya nodded. "Extremis alters the part of the brain that keeps a complete blueprint of the human body. When we're injured, we refer to that area of the brain in order to heal properly. Extremis rewrites the repair center."

She pulled out her phone now and scrolled through a series of icons to call up an image file. "Here, look at this photo. It's a chicken injected with an earlier version of the serum. This is the first stage, when the entire body essentially becomes an open wound. The normal body blueprint is being replaced with the Extremis blueprint, you see? The brain is being told that the body is wrong."

Tony was staring at Maya with his mouth open. She looked up at him, seemingly surprised, and stopped speaking.

"You injected a chicken with Super-Soldier Serum? Maya, that's…you are so weird. What were you going to do if you ended up with a super-chicken?"

Maya seemed startled. "We'd finished the mice trials, we were out of monkeys, and…it's what we had. Why? What do you experiment on?"

"Me."

"You'd better not be wrong, then."

"Sometimes I'm wrong. I get better."

"The chicken didn't." She flashed another photo. This one showed a red-eyed chicken encased in what looked like a bio-metallic cocoon that was rotting around the edges.

"Extremis protocol dictates that the subject be put on life support and intravenously fed nutrients just prior to the incubation phase. For the next two or three days, the subject remains unconscious within a cocoon of scabs."

She waved the photo one last time and said, "It's pretty gross, as you can imagine. Extremis uses the nutrients and body mass to build new organs. Better ones. We loaded in everything we could think of. The hypothetical we were given was to build a three-man team that could take Fallujah on its own."

Tony ran his hand through his hair and sat back. This was bad. "And this Extremis is what was stolen from Futurepharm? A super-soldier biological compiler? And someone took the serum *without* following your protocol. Survived, obviously. Could be unstable. Probably already was. And is now…what a mess.

"You're going to have to hand details of the process over to the authorities."

Maya winced. Tears started rolling down her cheeks. "It's my life's work, Tony. We were so close to success."

"Hey, Maya, easy." He stood up and walked over to her, put an arm around her. "You'll find something else. Look at me. One day, I'm making weapons, the next I'm completely reformed and out saving the world. And I'll help you. I've got some pull here and there. The authorities like me pretty well. I'll talk to them—maybe you can destroy Extremis instead of handing it over."

She looked up at Tony, shock across her face.

"So...destroy your life's work? Yeah, maybe that wasn't the right thing to say. I've got empathy down, but I'm still working on timing."

Tony put both arms around Maya now and drew her close. He could feel her warm, wet tears on his shoulder and wondered briefly whether they'd leave a stain on his suit. He could feel her shaking, heaving slightly as she tried to contain her emotions.

Her hair still smelled like apples.

He absentmindedly brought one hand up to her hair, stroking it while wondering about the chemical composition of the smell—thinking idly that one day, when he had some free time, he'd look into the science of creating smells. That might be useful to Stark Enterprises' appliance division, if they could figure out a way to introduce a hint of smell into certain appliances. Humidifiers, for example, or an in-house food composter that smelled nice.

Tony's cell phone buzzed, jarring him back into the moment. He realized he'd been holding Maya much longer and tighter than was appropriate for someone claiming to just be helping out a friend. He stepped back so he could reach into his pocket to pull out his phone, but Maya didn't release him. She tugged at him. Closer.

Tony remembered he liked apples. He reached down and pulled up Maya's chin so he could see her face. Her mascara had run down her cheeks, dripping from her tears. He wiped the smudges away, one side at a time.

"You're still so beautiful," he said, gently caressing her upper arms, then sliding his hands down to her waist.

She stretched up to reach his face and kissed him.

He let her, held her tighter, and stroked her back. She was barely larger than she had been when they'd first met, though he was sure her work schedule allowed for very little physical activity.

She probably skips a lot of meals, he realized.

And then they were kissing, first tentatively and then sloppily. Tony tried to think of all his resolutions to be a new man, to convince Pepper that he was done being a womanizer, and that she should take him seriously. But what if Pepper never loved him back? What if she always saw him as just a friend and boss?

Maya was smart and beautiful. Possibly a genius equal to Tony himself. Hadn't she just done the impossible, overwritten the human brain as if it were a hard drive in need of new software?

Smart is sexy, Tony thought.

She moved back, took his hand, pulled him toward the jet's sleeping quarters. He took a step toward her.

His phone buzzed again. He glanced down. *Mrs. Rennie.* He gently pushed Maya away. What was he doing?

"I have to take this."

"Tony…"

"Maya, no. I'm sorry. This is wrong. I've changed."

"People don't change, Tony."

"I have. I'm a better person now, and I'm not done changing yet."

She turned away as Tony voice-activated his phone.

"Mrs. Rennie. Why do you keep calling me?"

"Markko in Engineering has been trying to get you on the phone, Mister Stark. He claims it's extremely urgent. Something personal."

"Thank you, Mrs. Rennie. For everything."

"What?"

"Put him on...Markko! Stark here. You did? Excellent. I'm on the plane, so send—"

He waited a moment as Markko talked excitedly. "Okay, I'm listening. What have you got?"

As Tony listened, he glanced at Maya, who had her back to him. "Good job, Markko. I owe you dinner. That Greek place with the belly dancer you like. Yeah, I'll move you out of appliances for a while. Send the decrypted files to my secure personal server. I'll go through it when I get a chance. Nice work."

Tony had no time for subtlety. He turned to Maya.

"My guy hacked your dead boss's files. He gave Extremis to a group of militiamen south of Austin. Domestic terrorists."

Maya closed her eyes and covered her face with her hands.

"I have to make some calls," said Tony. "We're landing in a minute. Happy will drive you back to Futurepharm."

"You're not coming?"

"I'm going to find your super-soldier, Maya. You saw what he did at the FBI. Guns won't stop him. It's got to be me."

He left Maya alone and went into the next room, which was dark aside from a blue projection screen. "Initiate Iron Man warm-up sequence," said Tony. He used his fingerprint to unlock a storage panel that slid back, revealing his armor. "Next, access Avengers liaison channel. Priority A-1. Iron Man."

He paused a moment while the voice-recognition system cleared him. "Information regarding attack on FBI station, Houston. Forward to all relevant law enforcement entities. Upload of related files to follow ten seconds behind this message."

The projection screen now showed a diagram of the Iron Man armor and the words "Iron Man warm-up sequence engaged."

"Perpetrator of Houston attack is in superhuman aspect, possibly suffering side effects of process. Local law enforcement should not engage alone. Repeat, perpetrator is in superhuman aspect, do not engage alone or without further information. Perpetrator and associates likely to be in transit from Houston to Bastrop at this time. Details of superhuman aspect pending. Review files for background."

The Iron Man diagram was now glowing red. *Ready.*

"Iron Man is available for intercept and engagement."

Tony put the phone down, then spotted his reflection on the projection screen, superimposed over the Iron Man diagram.

He saw the future.

And this time, he didn't look away.

TEN

"Mallen, gimme a beer."

Mallen grunted something unintelligible from the back of the van. Beck turned around.

"Huh?"

"No more beer."

"Nilsen, pull off at the next exit. We need beer. Mallen, do you still drink, now that you're all...uh...?" Beck motioned at Mallen—whose appearance had transformed during his time in the slaughterhouse, from man to creature, then deceptively back to normal man—and shrugged.

"I can drink you under the table, Beck."

"You can't. You still owe me ten bucks for the last time you tried that."

"You wanna find out?"

Beck shook his head, demonstrating a bit of common sense for a change. "No. After what you did back there…Mallen, did you have to burn the whole building? We could've just gone after the guys that killed your—"

"Shut up, Beck. People that join the Feds make a choice."

"If we don't get beer soon, I'm going to make a choice, too. A choice to drive through the window of one of these crappy gas stations so we can get some beer. Why the hell does everything close so early here?" Nilsen had pulled off into a small Texas town that seemed to be little more than a rest area along the highway.

"Remember back at the group home," said Beck, "when we used to swipe beer from Old Man Cecil down at the guard shack?"

"No, *you* stole beer from Old Man Cecil. I used to hang with him. He was all right," said Mallen.

"You just liked him cuz he knew your dad."

"My dad used to make bets with him. Like telling him he'd give him his old Civil War musket if Cecil could skin a rabbit all in one piece." Mallen chuckled. "Cecil always lost."

"Like with you and my ten bucks."

"Shut up."

Beck shut up a lot faster now than he used to, Mallen noticed. There were fringe benefits to being the strongest, fastest, most invulnerable man in town. In the state? The country?

The world?

Mallen hadn't thought about his father's Enfield musket in years. He had wanted it, wondered where the Feds had taken it after the raid. No family possessions had come with him to the county shelter or the group home—or the first foster home, or the second or third. He'd been allowed nothing that belonged to his parents. The government took it all.

They took his parents, too.

Mallen had been ten years old, sitting on the floor playing with his .22—he'd just gotten it for his birthday—in the corner of the old cabin, when his father pulled up outside in the '57 Ford pickup.

His dad ran in, shouting. His mother, older brother, and uncle looked up from their poker game.

"It was a Goddamn trap! A *government* trap!"

"What?" said his mother. "ATF? FBI?"

"They were waiting for me to buy the guns. Hell, they were the ones selling me the guns! It was all I could do to get out of there! And then they followed me on to our property—"

"Are they here now?"

"I think...I think I killed one."

"Mr. Mallen." A voice over a bullhorn echoed through the cabin.

Ten-year-old Mallen checked his .22 to make sure it was loaded. He clicked the safety back and forth a few times. He'd never shot more than a bottle or a squirrel. Maybe that was gonna change today.

"Oh, God," said his mother. She grabbed and loaded her Winchester.

"Mr. Mallen, we've surrounded your property," came the bullhorn-voice again.

"See? Our property," said his brother as he reached up the cabin wall to unrack the Enfield. "This is entrapment. They lie to you, trespass...this ain't right, Pa. We're free people! They can't just lie to us because we scare 'em."

From Mallen's spot on the floor, he had a good view of his mother's calves below her skirt as she stepped over last night's leftover beer bottles on her way out the front door. She waved her rifle.

"Why don't you shove it right up your—"

The government's bullet went straight through his mother's head, exploding her skull and sending her brains splattering on to the cabin walls. His brother and uncle went next, baseball caps and hair drenched in blood. Finally, Dad was shot through the skull as he cradled Mom's head.

Mallen had wished many times that he'd run outside with his .22 that day, a ten-year-old fighting with honor before going down in a hail of Federal bullets. He'd never have had to move from foster home to foster home, never have been returned over and over to the group home like an unwanted holiday gift or defective appliance being sent back to the store. But instead of running outside, young Mallen had stayed crouched against the wall.

Much as he was crouched against the side of the van today.

"You okay, Mallen? You were making some noises," said Nilsen from the driver's seat.

"Fine," said Mallen. He looked up at the top of the van. He wasn't going to stay crouched this time. "Just fine."

"Good," said Beck. "Because we're going to drive a few more miles up to the next exit, and then I'll need your ten bucks. Unless you want me to steal the beer."

From above, the van didn't look suspicious. Iron Man watched it pull back on to the interstate.

"I'm streaming you video from my cameras. Confirm that as the vehicle identified from surveillance footage?"

"That's a confirm, Iron Man," said a crackly voice from highway patrol headquarters. "Only gray 1990 Econoline in the region. Sorry it took all afternoon to find—we were looking west on I-10 until a trooper called in the missing plates. They're coming up on the off-ramp."

"Understood," said Tony from inside his Iron Man armor. "Jarvis, toggle to thermal-imaging scope and fix on target."

Iron Man's video feed switched to hazy infrared. He could pick out shapes inside the van now.

"Okay…one driver, one front passenger…very hot spot in the back…that's our boy. That's a lock."

Iron Man sped up a little and arced across the evening sky. He felt omnipotent when he was flying, and there was no better use for the Iron Man armor than protecting innocents.

"I'm going to engage the vehicle on the off-ramp when it's isolated from other traffic," Iron Man explained to highway patrol via radio. "I'll be using repulsor weapons. These are reactionless force protection—one-way push. Get in the way of one, and you're risking broken bones and internal organ damage. I want all police officers pulled back until I've subdued the target. You'll be responsible for the two men in the front. I'll free them up for you. Do not approach the man in the back under any circumstances. He can only be taken down by my repulsors, not by regular ammunition. Stand by."

Tony switched off his two-way radio and voice-activated his armor munitions. "Jarvis, set repulsors at 40 percent. That should be enough for this. Don't want to vaporize the two accomplices."

Glowing circles on Iron Man's palms fired up into white plasma; like lasers, two repulsors streaked through the sky toward the Econoline. The repulsors swiftly and neatly sliced the van in half. The front of the van, carrying the driver and one passenger, careened down the off-ramp on two wheels, sparking wildly as it swerved toward the guardrail and the waiting state troopers.

The rear of the van veered erratically and somersaulted off the exit ramp, flipping twice before it crashed to a stop amid a storm of debris.

A figure emerged from the steaming wreckage. Mallen was unhurt, but was roaring and furious. Whatever Maya's serum had done to the man, he didn't look all that different from any other enraged person. He appeared mostly average, if average had a temper and was wandering around the highway having a really bad day.

"Target. Zoom in," said Iron Man. His optical zoom bracketed the man on the ground and brought him into sharp focus. Jeans. Leather coat. T-shirt. Average height and weight, Caucasian male in his mid-30s, short brown hair. But wait. Tony frowned and zoomed in closer. His eyes…his teeth. The man's gums and irises had a coppery sheen to them. And the look on his face—the clenched, exposed teeth, the tense, furrowed brow, the slitted eyes. He looked vicious, like a killer in attack mode.

Iron Man hovered, then landed on the ground. He extended his arm toward Mallen, palm out, repulsor glowing white.

"Lay down on your face with your hands behind you and cross your ankles," said Iron Man. "There's no reason this has to be difficult."

Mallen's face contorted with rage. His hands were clenched.

"Yes, there is," said Mallen. "Ask your FBI friends what they did to the Mallen family and then you'll see. *Lots* of reasons."

Fine, thought Tony. He hit Mallen with a repulsor.

Mallen absorbed it in a fiery glow. He moved slowly forward, inconvenienced but not overwhelmed, as if pushing through a pile of fresh snow. Tony saw Mallen's jaw relax a bit.

"Increase repulsor to 80 percent, Jarvis," said Tony. He blasted Mallen again, with no effect.

Okay, thought Tony. *This is surprising.*

Mallen ducked away from Iron Man's barrage. *How?* He leapt aside as Tony followed, blasting only dirt and grass with his repulsor. *Damn, he's fast.*

Then Mallen was there, right in front of Iron Man. He blasted Tony with flames, heating up the armor on the right side.

"All systems to 100 percent," said Tony, confirming his power levels visually on the internal-armor holographic display. "We'll do this the hard way."

He grabbed Mallen by the throat, choking off his flames and lifting his feet off the ground.

"You're under arrest," said Iron Man.

Mallen felt his air being cut off as his fiery breath turned into red mist, evaporating into flames spewing from his open mouth. His fire had no effect on Iron Man's fire-repellent armor. He started to choke, then felt a tingle in his left hand.

Claw-like electrodes, sparking blue, extended from his fingers.

Huh, he thought. *Didn't know I could do that.*

Mallen's powers appeared to be evolving.

He grabbed Iron Man's forearm and sunk his claws into the armor. He felt them penetrate the outer shield, then watched as an electric charge jolted through billionaire Tony Stark, electrocuting and short-circuiting the armor.

Iron Man crackled and fell.

"Rich jackass can't even stand up in that costume without power," snarled Mallen. "Here, let me help you."

He swiftly lifted the seemingly lifeless figure over his head, then threw Iron Man. Threw the weight of the Iron Man armor and the man inside, with no more effort than a kid would toss a softball.

Mallen watched as Iron Man receded to a dark speck in the sky.

The Iron Man armor flatlined across Tony's in-helmet holographic displays. The Heads-Up Display sparked and vanished, along with his ocular controls and Jarvis. That left Tony Stark alone and merely human inside what had become, for the moment, a worthless, heavy shell.

Extremis appeared to be rewriting Mallen's abilities on the fly. At the FBI, it had granted him superhuman strength and fire-breathing capabilities. Here it extruded claw-like electrodes, emitting an electrical field specifically adapted to interrupting its opponent's—Iron Man's—armor. Extremis was a biological weapon, not hampered by the same limits as traditional AI. Was it gradually giving Mallen unlimited powers, or just adapting to whatever threat was at hand?

And now Tony was flying, but this wasn't the sort of flying he enjoyed. He was flung, powerless, through the sky, protected only by the strength of the Iron Man suit's armor alloy.

"Restart." The Iron Man armor had an auto-reboot

function built-in, but the electric shock had delayed it. The only thing working in his armor at the moment was the bit of Velcro he'd taped under the eye guard for when he had to scratch his nose.

"Any time now. Jarvis?"

Iron Man could see the interstate below him. He was going to crash down in the middle of the westbound passing lane. Tony clicked the emergency power button by his left thumb a few times, with no results.

The word RESTART slowly fizzled into view on the HUD. The armor began to come online.

But not in time.

Iron Man crash-landed on to the hood of a silver, four-door sedan racing down the highway at sixty-five miles per hour. The front windshield, skylight, and driver's side window shattered, and the car's steel front undercarriage hit the asphalt as the rear went airborne. A boxy red hatchback screeched in under the rear of the sedan, crumpling under the weight as the first car pivoted back down. The two cars slid together to a halt, and Iron Man tumbled off the sedan and on to the pavement. He had regained power now, and leapt to his feet.

"Oh, God," said Iron Man as a third driver lost control, this car flipping into the air over the two that had already crashed.

The third car crashed into another. Both exploded in a ball of fire that engulfed the interstate. No one walked away.

How many had just died?

TONY STARK FAILS.

The headlines tomorrow would not be kind. The vicious personal attack on Pepper would be nothing compared to this—and this time, it was the truth.

Then Mallen arrived, leaping clear across the highway to land crouched on two legs and a fist. The road shuddered, and the pavement buckled under the impact.

Iron Man wasn't at 100 percent yet—Tony confirmed this on his HUD. But he had power and ocular systems. And he wasn't holding back this time.

Tony scanned his available munitions. *Ah. Screamers.*

"Forty-five seconds, Jarvis."

Iron Man's armor emitted a directional screeching alarm. An ordinary man would have lost balance, collapsed, and bled from the ears, struck down with immediate hearing damage. Mallen covered his ears with his hands and grimaced. He rocked from side to side for a moment.

Iron Man pulled back his fist for a blow that would kill a normal man.

Too late. Mallen reached out his right arm and stopped Iron Man's fist in mid-punch. He caught and held it. *Impossible*, thought Tony. *The man's eardrums should be nearly vaporized. He shouldn't even be able to stand.* Had he grown new eardrums on the spot?

Mallen's fist tightened around Tony's right hand, crushing it through the armor.

"AAAAAAAA!" Iron Man fired a hundred microbursts from his shoulder arsenal. They exploded all around Mallen's head, like tiny land mines. Mallen grimaced and screamed in pain.

And then he smiled as he recovered. He kicked Iron Man's right knee backward, instantly snapping the ligaments, destroying the cartilage, and crushing the joint.

Iron Man's hand and leg were held together now by just the armor. He swung his left arm around and fired a repulsor at Mallen's face with all the power left in his weapons system.

Scarred and battered, Mallen sneered through broken teeth and swung a punch directly at Iron Man's heart.

Tony stumbled, saw flecks of his own blood through his helmet. The words TORSO UNIT BREACH flashed across his HUD. His lungs and heart ached. His armor compromised, his organs failing, Tony knew now he could not win against Maya's invention. She'd built a better weapon, one that evolved by learning and reacting to his every attack.

As Iron Man fell weakly to his knees, Mallen strode over to a black car, a car carrying a family. He punched his fists through the hood, grabbing the holes he'd made as if they were handles.

He lifted the car—with three innocents inside, panicked and screaming—high above his head, high over the nearly useless Iron Man.

TONY STARK FAILS.

I'm not going to be around to see that headline, thought Tony.

ELEVEN

"Alert: Sensors indicate shallow breathing and rapid pulses of three passengers within civilian vehicle elevated directly overhead."

"Thanks for the update, Jarvis," said Tony. "How are we doing locally?"

"Iron Man armor breached at copolymer ballistic joinery between torso strike face and nanocomposite shoulder panels. Laminate is cracked on all major surfaces. Excessive blood loss approaching class II hemorrhage with reduction by mechanical compression and emergency suture application on right leg, right hand, and upper chest. Right knee musculoskeletal damage is acute, with potentially irreversible bone and cartilage trauma. Use is not currently recommended. Containment structure of right hand has been destroyed, but temporary splintage has been accomplished by Iron Man gauntlet. Warning: Splintage may lead to immobility and potentially to further damage."

"What's the good news?"

"Painkillers are online, containment sub-skin is activated. Kinetic energy threshold statistics have been recorded and uploaded to Stark Enterprises R&D department for use in future laboratory research."

"Swell. I'll keep that in mind if we ever make it back to the lab," said Tony from his crumpled, semi-kneeling position on the wrecked interstate surface. He stared up at Mallen, who towered over him, dominant, straining slightly under the effort of holding the black sedan above his head. Mallen's face was scarred, and his teeth were broken from Iron Man's seedpod bomblet assault. His leather coat was shredded and burned. But Mallen himself was unharmed, aside from being walking rage, a furious vessel of violent wrath.

Iron Man weakly held up his uninjured arm in front of his body, in the shadow of the car. Pointless, he knew, but he was semi-delirious from painkillers, and self-protection was an instinct. He felt helpless, feeble with his broken bones and damaged armor, but somehow he had to stop Mallen from hurting the three people in the car. Tony analyzed the situation as quickly as he could in his medicated haze, trying to find an advantage of intellect and experience over this psychotic Extremis enhancile.

"All the money in the world can't change that you're just a weak, pathetic human under that shiny shell," said Mallen. "You're inferior. Pitiful. Not like me. I'm a real man, with real strength and power. You're going to burst inside that suit when this car hits you. They're going to have to pour you out."

The harder they come, thought Tony. "Jarvis, route all power including life support on my mark."

"Diverting power from life-support systems at this time is not recommended."

"Shut up and do it." Tony scanned his holographic body-data output as pain-killing functions temporarily ceased. He began to feel new aches, intensifying rapidly.

I can stand this, he thought. He had to. Tony Stark could be crushed, Iron Man destroyed, but three more innocent deaths on Tony's watch were unbearable. "Power divert. Chest beam. NOW!"

A massive, blinding-white uni-beam shot straight out of Iron Man's arc reactor, catching Mallen directly in the chest with the force of an anti-tank missile. Mallen vanished in a swift blur, the beam's impact battering him, sending him flying a half-mile away.

Iron Man anchored himself stiffly on his remaining useful leg and held up both arms to catch and brace the car as it fell.

"Oh, hell…" said Tony, as the car crashed down on him. He was inside the most advanced technological system on earth, and his research hadn't accounted for being outmatched. This wasn't supposed to happen. He wasn't supposed to be merely a fragile human with an unpowered shell, little more than a turtle with thumbs, overcome by weight and simple physics. He felt the highway under his boots shudder and crack.

The sheer weight of the Iron Man armor held the car momentarily. The civilians above would survive this experience, as long as Tony could just lower the car gradually to the ground.

"Reroute all available power back to normal armor functions," wheezed Tony as the car weighed down on him.

"Power transmission is at zero percent," said Jarvis. Tony's HUD confirmed this.

"No no no. Don't you dare. Auxiliary power: activate. Anything."

Then, joint by joint, Tony heard the armor split and fracture as the strain overcame him. First the elbow guards, then the shoulder plates, and finally the neck joints hissed and cracked as his pressurized containment layer fragmented. Iron Man folded up and collapsed under the car, crushed into the pavement. The damaged vehicle landed on top of him with a thud.

"Auxiliary power on: Iron Man safe mode," reported Jarvis cheerfully.

Thank God, thought Tony. Another fail-safe activated. Plus, the painkillers were back online. *Now to get this car off me without scaring the passengers any more than they are already.*

And that's when Iron Man noticed a sudden change in temperature—*it's getting kinda warm in here,* he thought—and the orange-and-yellow flickering of flames creeping up to encircle the car.

......

Mallen plummeted to the ground with a tremendous THUMP a half-mile east along the highway. The pavement cracked as he slammed down and skidded thirty feet before grinding to a halt in a crater of coarse asphalt and tar.

"Ufff."

Mallen raised himself up on one knee and pressed a hand to his chest where the uni-beam had struck him. His heart thudded with pressure, and he felt faintly disoriented. He stopped for a moment, hesitating, catching his breath.

"Oww. You bastard..." Mallen stood up slowly, cautiously, and let the dizzy spell subside. His head hurt, and his pulse thudded in his skull with a booming echo throughout his limbs and body.

Iron Man had hurt him, and Mallen felt it in every muscle and nerve. But more important: Mallen had nearly *killed* Iron Man. He'd crushed Iron Man's leg and hand, cracked open his expensive suit with almost no effort. Iron Man's bombs had little effect on him.

Ruined my coat, Mallen thought, glancing with annoyance at the holes in his old leather jacket.

Mallen could easily take out Iron Man any time he wanted.

How about now?

Then Mallen realized the thudding in his skull wasn't the sound of his heart. It was the steady, rhythmic pulse of helicopter blades and rotors slicing through the air. A squadron of state-police choppers were approaching the scene. Five of them, almost directly overhead.

Mallen could have fought and downed them all without any real danger to himself, he now knew. But he was bruised and breathless from his battle with Iron Man. And anyway, his beef was with the Feds, not the cops. His goal wasn't to kill the *most* people. It was to kill the *right* people.

Iron Man is a tool of the government, he told himself. *Helps them suppress free will. Doesn't matter, though. Not important. I'll get back to him later if I need to. All the time in the world now. Leave the little things behind.*

Another thing he was leaving behind was Beck and Nilsen. Last he'd seen them, they'd been sliding down the highway in half a van. The cops had probably taken them in, he knew. If they had any sense, they'd say he'd forced them to drive him around, and maybe they'd get off with probation or a year of house arrest.

Or maybe he should find them, rip them free from their restraints and bring them along. But they were just normal humans, inferior to him. They'd only hold him back. And probably be pissed at him for being better than them now.

"I hope those two losers get their beer," said Mallen. He turned away from the scene on the highway and ran.

Trapped by the car and flames, Tony thought he saw Mallen run. But his vision was blurry through his unpowered visor, a haze of fire, and specks of his own blood that dotted the Iron Man helmet. The flames danced closer, swirling along trails of escaped fuel, until Iron Man's entire field of vision was a fiery red and the suit felt like a furnace.

"Jarvis! Secondary systems. NOW."

The words AUXILIARY POWER ON/IRON MAN SAFE MODE faded into view and flashed twice on Tony's holographic display. He tried again to push the car up and away, but his right arm was useless and his left arm was only human-powered now.

"Come on. Come on." The family in the car that imprisoned Tony was screaming above him.

"Mommy, Mommy! The fire is coming this way—!"

"I know! The doors are jammed shut! Oh, God— the heat!"

The temperature rose as Iron Man watched the fire lick the edges of his armor. The suit's alloys were fire-repellent, but life support was barely online at the moment and the armor wasn't supplying oxygen. Tony coughed and wheezed. He needed air or he'd suffocate.

THERMOCOUPLE/HEAT-INDUCTIVE TRANSFER FIELD ONLINE. Tony could breathe again. Finally, life support and secondary systems were back.

"Jarvis, give me energy from those flames," he said. He could feel Iron Man's power increasing as his electromagnets recharged, slowly transferring particles from the air around him. *Primitive,* he thought, *but effective.* Iron Man extended his mangled right arm, the armor giving it the structure and power he needed.

"Recirculate internal plasma," he said as he arced his arm, sucking in energy. His armor recycled the surrounding blaze, creating a safe perimeter around the car.

HEAT-POWER TRANSFER SUCCESSFUL. POWER AT 1%.

"I don't feel very successful," said Tony. "I feel like I've just been beaten to a pulp by an angry idiot." He slowly pushed the car up off the ground and swiveled it over, then lowered it down safely to one side. "Jarvis, activate police-band communications. Iron Man to all points: I'm going to be *immobilized* in about a minute and a half." He coughed. "Could use some...*cough*... immediate aid."

An alert popped up on his HUD. MEDICAL/ SUIT EMERGENCY-INTERVENTION SYSTEM AUTO-ACTIVATING. SEEK URGENT MEDICAL ASSISTANCE.

"Well, that's a huge help," said Tony. He closed his eyes, thought about the families of the people who had died here today. He thought of his own bruised and damaged body, and wondered whether he should try to get Pepper on the line to tell her he was critically injured. But he wasn't sure what time zone she was in, and she'd just worry anyway, so he lay still and waited instead.

A minute later, a paramedic stood over him. "How do I check your vital signs?" Firefighters were tackling the nearby blaze and seemed to have it under control, and ambulances had arrived to help the injured.

"You don't have to," explained Iron Man. "My armor records an in-depth report of anything wrong with me. In short: Everything is broken. I have pulverized bones, excessive bleeding, and internal injuries. It's as if

I've been Hulk-smashed. And the piece of Velcro I use to scratch my nose is missing."

"You want me to…?"

"No, no. An itchy nose takes my mind off my other problems. Where…is he?"

"He took off on foot," said the paramedic. "We clocked him at three hundred miles an hour moving east. What about you? All that damage…do we call your office or the Avengers or…?"

"I've already transmitted briefings on my condition and the potential risks of the situation. Use one of your choppers. I need an airlift. I can't take the armor off—it's got me immobilized, and it's all that's holding me together. And not too many bumps in the ride, please. I'm bleeding too much as it is…and scrubbing blood out of this thing…is a pain…"

"Where do we take you? The hospital?"

"No," said Iron Man. "Take me to Futurepharm."

Tony closed his eyes and spoke to his AI. "Jarvis, sedatives, please. Maintain all compression and pain-killers, and knock me out until we're back in Austin." Tony heard EMTs and state police yelling instructions over him as his world faded from view.

TWELVE

The crackling of feet on dry leaves woke Mallen before sunrise. He leapt to his feet on the porch of the old Arkansas hunting cabin, ready for a fight.

A white-tailed deer froze in the clearing in front of the cabin. A young buck, Mallen realized, not a threat. For a moment, he thought about grabbing and choking the deer—he hadn't eaten since yesterday afternoon, before Houston—but butchering the animal would be difficult without a knife or saw and would make a huge mess. Also, Mallen didn't yet know whether there were cooking supplies in the cabin. He was easily strong enough to take down a deer with his bare hands, but there was more straightforward prey—fast food and convenience stores—along his route.

"Try me again if I'm still here in a week," said Mallen to the deer. It stood for a minute, blinking its big brown eyes, then fled into the forest.

Mallen swung his arms back and forth twice, twisted his shoulders a few times, then shook his stiff legs. Apparently, the ability to sleep comfortably on wooden planks wasn't one of his new super-powers. He hadn't thought about that when he'd stopped a few hours after dark, exhausted from his day of sorting out the Houston FBI, and then an evening of testing and honing his new skills against that so-called Iron Man.

"Should've stopped at the Motel 6," he muttered. But that wouldn't have made any sense, he realized. Mallen needed to be far beyond the reach of irritating authorities and nosy hotel workers.

He kicked the locked cabin door open with a casual thump of his boot and headed straight to the kitchenette. Nothing but a can of deviled ham and some Vienna sausages. *Gross. Raw deer might've been better.* He shrugged. This would do for the moment. He'd hit a Denny's when he got to the next town.

When Tony woke up a little more than an hour later, he heard the speed of the helicopter blade-slap change and groggily realized he'd arrived back in Austin. He swung in the wind, still locked in his armor, dangling from the helicopter like a piece of construction equipment.

The propeller slowed and the wind changed as the chopper hovered, then lowered Iron Man on to the industrial-strength motorized utility cart in the Futurepharm parking lot. His external video monitors showed him three lab techs in white coats and earplugs surrounding the cart. They unfastened hooks and cables, freeing him from the copter.

And then there was Maya, pointing and barking orders as the helicopter lifted skyward.

"Sorry it's not a proper bariatric gurney," said Maya, standing above Iron Man's head and torso. "But I was afraid your armor's weight would collapse it. We use this for moving heavy equipment around."

"That's okay, Maya. I *am* heavy equipment."

She moved to take off his helmet.

"No...Maya...lift the visor, but not the helmet. My armor won't come off until I deactivate medical protocols. And I can't yet...it's all that's keeping me alive."

"What? We need to get you to a hospital."

"No...you have...unique medical facilities," said Tony. "And this..." He paused.

"This is about Extremis."

Mallen was a blur of dust, streaking across green-and-amber fields on his way through Arkansas. As he approached the outskirts of a small town, he slowed to a walk.

A teenage girl leaned back under a speed-limit sign alongside the village's main road. She sat on a milk crate reading the morning news on a small tablet computer, her black-denim-covered legs stretched out in front of her.

TONY STARK FAILS, screamed the headline.

The girl tried to light a cigarette as Mallen approached.

She struggled with the match a second time and coughed. "Jeez…" She looked up at Mallen, her short, spiky, jet-black hair and multiple ear piercings partly in his shadow.

"What're you looking at?" She was trying to appear intimidating and unapproachable behind her long, black leather coat and plum-colored lipstick.

"Nothing," said Mallen. He stood above her.

"I come out here to smoke, okay? No one around to bug me or say no." She coughed again.

Mallen hadn't meant to threaten the girl. She reminded him of a girl from one of his foster homes. Probably the closest he'd had to a sister. At least, they'd fought like they were related. "It's okay," he said. "I'm just passing through."

She gave him a withering glance and looked away. Her gentle demeanor detracted from her attempted toughness.

"Keep going," she said. "I come out here to be on my own. The crap I get in town. I need some time alone."

Mallen stooped down so she didn't have to look up into the sun to see his face. He wondered what she made of the deep scars he now bore from his battle with Iron Man. Her black steel-toed boots, he noticed, were carefully oiled. She worked hard on her appearance. Like Nilsen's kid, the one in junior high. Would old Nilsen ever get his kids back, now that he'd probably been arrested?

"Got an extra cigarette?"

……

"Get him into the medical lab on sublevel 2! Go!" Maya barked orders at the Futurepharm lab techs. "Park him there and leave. This is classified—*no one* is to speak to the press. Refer any reporters' inquiries to me, then tell them I'm not available. I'll take it from here."

The technicians wheeled the gurney carrying Iron Man into the lab, handed Maya the utility cart's remote control, and backed away. She swiped her keycard through the pad to secure the door, then turned to look at her patient.

"That Extremis process of yours…it's pretty good, you know," Tony wheezed softly.

"I saw the news. He did this to you?"

"Incredible speed. Moved faster than I could operate the armor. And he gets better as he goes: Extremis evolves, has all the characteristics of machine-learning software— emergent tech, adapting with experience. All right, let's get started. Jarvis: Deactivate emergency medical containment."

The armor beeped and released with a hydraulic hiss.

"Now, Maya, lift my chest piece off."

She grunted with the strain. "Damn, this is heavy."

"Saved my life, I think," said Tony. "I'm pretty messed up."

"You should be in a hospital," said Maya.

"I heard you the first time. Now get the boots. I gave some thought to the hospital…while I had a car on top of me. Hospitals are fine for most people, but they don't have the thing I need."

"And what's that? Oh, God." Maya pulled off the Iron Man shin guard. Blood poured out of it and on to the gurney. "Your leg's a mess. How were you still standing?"

"I wasn't. Armor…injected me with painkillers. I can't feel it. And I'll be even better…once you shoot me up…with a reconfigured Extremis dose." Tony coughed.

Maya stopped pulling off his armor and stared at him.

"You've gone insane."

"He's a biological combat machine, Maya…and I'm just a man in a weaponized alloy suit. I've spent months in my garage trying to increase the armor's response time. Gotten as fast as is mechanically possible. And it's still. Not. Fast. Enough."

Tony turned his head and looked straight at Maya now. "I need to wire the armor directly into my brain. Extremis can do that."

"Tony. No."

"Maybe we could work in some kind of Tivo thing while we're at it. My board would love that. Brain television."

Maya didn't laugh. "Extremis is untested," she said. "Even its current configuration—"

"Seems to work fine. Just look at my face," finished Tony.

"And the guy was presumably healthy when he took the dose. *You* look like you've been pushed through a wood chipper," said Maya.

"Still wanna kiss me?" He puckered his lips and made

smoochy sounds. Maya recoiled. Tony laughed, but it turned into a throaty gurgle. He gasped and recovered. "Extremis works through the healing center, you said. It'll accelerate my recovery while it's giving me an upgrade."

She pulled off his right gauntlet. His hand had been crushed; blood spilled out of the glove. Maya quickly stretched a bandage around Tony's hand and leaned forward, applying pressure.

"I don't need the powers," Tony continued. "The strength, the weapons—I have them. Best there are. Built them myself. And I don't feel a compelling need to breathe fire. If anything, we're talking about simplifying the payload. I need to *be* the suit. I'm not trying to grow new organs, though a new liver might help with the damage I did in my younger years. I want to grow new connections…

"This thing, my armor, it's gotten too heavy. And too slow. I'm talking about speed of deployment…speed of operation…"

"Tony…" Maya stood back now, gesturing at his crumpled, bloody right hand.

"Thank God for painkillers, eh?" He smiled. "Get a computer in here. Let's get to work, before I pass out."

"They give you trouble around here?" Mallen lit the teenager's cigarette for her.

"I like black clothes. I like a certain kind of music. I have a vocabulary of more than ten words," she said. "What do you think?"

"Yeah, I was different when I was your age, too."

"I swear," she said. "Wear a long coat and everyone thinks you're a psycho-killer. I'm on suspension."

"I bet that went over well with your folks," said Mallen.

"My mother didn't mind so much, but her husband… man. He went ballistic. He doesn't even want me here. But my mom has custody, y'know?"

"Where's your dad?"

"Knoxville. He sent me back to mom after I came home from school with bleach splatters on my jeans and a Godzilla tattoo."

"That sounds cool to me." Mallen knelt down next to her, leaning his elbow on his knee. She finally offered a cigarette. He took it, then accepted a light. "No one wanted me, either. I always got thrown back, like a trout that's too small. And I got in a lot of fights."

"Did that get you suspended?"

"Nah," said Mallen. "Everybody else was fighting, too. I got suspended for arguing with history teachers and showing off my replica weapons. They were just models, couldn't even hurt anyone. Didn't make any damn sense. Oh, and once I got thrown out for sharing my lighter fluid with the younger kids on the playground, but it was no big deal. Teachers were just jealous they couldn't sniff it during school hours like I did. What'd you do?"

"Wrote a story in class about zombies attacking the town. They ate the city council. Then they ate the mayor. That's my mother's husband."

Mallen chuckled. For a minute, he considered killing the mayor as a favor, but that would piss off this girl's mother and probably make her situation even worse. Better to leave it. If the girl wanted to kill the mayor later, nothing was stopping her.

She continued. "They called it 'terroristic writing.' As if my zombie story could incite someone to do something they didn't already plan on doing. *Hmph*. This country's gone insane."

She took a long, hard drag on her cigarette and coughed again, just a little this time.

"I know exactly what you mean," said Mallen, leaning forward now. "What I don't get is, cops and Feds can just kill us—but if we even think about defending ourselves, that's called terrorism."

"See my T-shirt?" The girl sat up on the milk crate now. She opened her long leather jacket to reveal the shirt underneath. The American flag was emblazoned across her chest. Mallen grinned. This girl was cute for her age, a young patriot who wasn't going to follow the government's changing rules without a fight.

Then he looked closer and frowned. The flag contained a swastika instead of a field of stars. The gray lettering above the flag on the black background said "AmeriKKKa."

"What's that supposed to mean?" Mallen spoke icily now. He leaned back, away from the girl. "Is that how you see America?"

"Sure," she answered. "A country of white men pushing around the rest of us. And now those men are trying to go back to old-fashioned values, the kind that kept women in the kitchen, immigrants working on railroads, and only white people in the seat of power."

Mallen glowered at her. "You know, the Klan did good things, too. They defended Christian law in a lot of places."

She furrowed her brow and stared at him now. Challenged him, just like his foster sister used to before he'd hit her in the mouth.

"I'm so sick of hearing about God all the time," she said. "I'm sick of having to, like, pass a religion test just to live here. The Klan *lynched* people who didn't look like regular white folks."

Mallen stood up and tossed his cigarette down on the road. He ground it with his boot heel and leaned forward. This conversation had started to remind him of the discussions he used to have with his history teachers, right before they gave him detention.

"Regular white folks built this country," he said sternly. "Without government or spies or regulation or people with badges who kill your family for fun."

"Yeah." She wasn't backing down. "Except regular white folks did all that, too."

"Don't say that," said Mallen. He wanted to help her understand, but she wasn't making it easy. No one had ever listened to him, either, but that was changing now. "It all went wrong. I'm going to fix it. I've got this stuff in me, see? From the future they were going to make. But I stole it, and I'm using it to turn back the clock."

She pointed at him and leaned in, close enough to his face that he could feel her spitting.

"Back to lynchings and giving smallpox-infected blankets to different-looking people? Back to women being second-class citizens? You ever notice they're called Founding Fathers, with no mothers among them? You're as bad as them. Go away. Leave me alone."

He did leave her alone then. But first, he punched her. Hard. Right in the face. Hard enough that her head exploded. Like you'd kill a zombie if one invaded your town.

Her lifeless body jerked and fell with a thud, sideways to the yellowing grass along the shoulder of the road. Her head—what was left of it—hit the pavement and splattered.

The red of her bloodied brain oozed from the cavity that had been her skull. It stood out, contrasting starkly against the black of the asphalt, of her coat, jeans, and hair.

THIRTEEN

"I cleared the section and killed the CCTV," said Maya. Tony sat in a wheelchair now, holding his helmet in his lap, wearing only his blood-stained polymer circuit-skin. Maya rolled him down the hallway toward the Extremis research lab. "Can I talk you out of this? I mean, couldn't the Avengers or someone deal with him? You don't even know where he's gone."

"Yes, I do," said Tony. "I know exactly where he's going, I won't survive without Extremis, and FYI, I *am* an Avenger."

Maya wheeled Tony to one side of the lab door and handed him a card. She stepped over to the other side.

"Takes two people to open the Extremis vault. You use Killian's keycard. Wait for me...ready?"

Tony tried Killian's keycard a split second ahead of Maya, and the doors stayed shut.

"No, Tony. Same time. Are you okay?"

He looked tired. His face was pale.

"Other than being in a dizzy painkiller daze, Maya, sure, I'm doing great. Sorry. I can do it. This time, point to me when you're ready. Okay? Let's try again."

They both swiped their keycards simultaneously. The doors slid open. Inside, Tony saw monitors, keyboards, sensors, and a convertible reclining chair that doubled as an operating table.

"Very cozy," said Tony.

"All set up to run an Extremis process we never used," answered Maya.

"Well, you will now."

Maya's phone buzzed. "Excuse me," she said. "Maya Hansen here. Oh, yes. I'll be right there." She clicked off. "How much money do you spend on planes? A package has arrived from your office. I'll be right back. We'll start you on tube feeding when I return."

"Mmm, sounds tasty."

"Lay back on that chair and make yourself comfortable. If you can, I mean, given that you feel nothing."

She left the room. Tony slowly lifted himself out of the wheelchair and on to the operating table. He leaned over to one of the computers nearby, browsed through some files about Extremis, punched a few keys and scanned the results, then used his left hand to pull a retractable cable out of his Iron Man helmet. He plugged it into a monitor.

The words IRON MAN HUD PLAYBACK flashed across the screen, superimposed over a video recording of his point of view of Iron Man's fight with Mallen. Tony watched his repulsor beam slice the Econoline in half, then he zoomed in on Mallen inside the van's back section as it tumbled off the interstate exit ramp.

"Magnify top-left quadrant. Times 100. More. Zoom. Zoom. There." A road map lay half unfolded inside the van, to Mallen's left.

"That's how I know where you're going," said Tony aloud. The monitor lit up with a map of the southern United States, with an interstate route mapped out from Houston to Washington, D.C. "If I need three days to process Extremis, you'll be there before me. Even without the van." He turned back to the keyboard, tapped out a sequence, and studied the results some more.

Tony choked again and spat up more blood. "God…that's disgusting."

Maya returned, holding a case. "This is it?" She stood silhouetted in the doorway.

"Yeah, experimental unit. Bring it over here," said Tony. "I've been trying to get the Iron Man back to a collapsible model, but the more I add to it…it's overcomplicated, you know?"

Maya set the case down on a table next to the recliner. Tony opened the lock with his left-index fingerprint, and the case sprang open to reveal a collapsed portable Iron Man suit.

"This version is made out of memory metals and single-crystal titanium, custom-grown. An electric charge makes it snap into shape. And the molecular structure collimates into super-hard planes. Most of the interior elements compress to about 90 percent of their working volume.

"It's tougher and faster than the current unit. But I couldn't miniaturize the control systems. I still needed the undersheath, the hard upper torso, and the helmet system.

"We can reconfigure Extremis to do all those jobs. Make me Iron Man inside and out." He snapped the case shut.

Maya punched a code into a console. She wouldn't look at Tony.

"Or kill you," she said. "This is our last live dose, here in the Extremis compiler. We have to instruct the compiler what to do to you. The computer will recompile the dose—reprogram what it does. One mistake, and it *will* kill you."

"Well, let's not make any mistakes," said Tony. He tried to stand up, to see what Maya was doing at the compiler. "You better type. I'm down to one hand…"

He collapsed, and the world went black. Some time later—he didn't know how long—Maya faded back into view. She was standing above him.

"Tony?"

He vomited blood, then sat still for a minute. "The rest of the package—the nutrients and suspended metals—you know what I want to do with them?"

"Tony," said Maya quietly. "There's no way in hell you're going to survive an Extremis dose."

He looked up at her. "I have to," he said. "Or my internal injuries are going to kill me."

She helped move him back on to the operating table, then pulled off his circuit-skin shirt.

Tony winced. "So that's how it feels to not be fed a constant drip of painkillers." His knee was still getting local anesthesia, but before too long, his hand would be in excruciating pain and his chest would start to ache.

"You can still not do this," said Maya as she applied electrodes to Tony's chest. She used a hypodermic needle to puncture one of the veins in his working arm and began intravenous fluid-replacement therapy. "Call the Avengers."

"No, Maya. This is my fight to finish. No one else will understand the level of threat, and I'm the only one who can handle him."

She raised her eyebrows with skepticism. "I doubt that."

"Look," he explained. "Anyone else will make the same mistake I made. Overconfidence. He's far more dangerous than he looks because Extremis is still evolving. I don't want the death of an Avenger on my hands."

"Tony, you said he's going to Washington. For God's sake, at least warn them."

"If I die on the table, you warn them. Contact number is in my phone. Phone's in my armor. The PIN is 0000."

"Really, Tony? Why not just make it 'password'?"

"Cut me some slack. You know it's a new phone. I just got it on the way down here." He laid his head back now.

"Maya, this is what I do. All I have is making the future and stopping the animals who want to take the future away from people. This muck of yours is the future. It shouldn't be wasted on killers. You know that. They all need to see that, and so do I. Are the bags hooked up?"

"Tony, if we've made even one mistake in the compiling…"

"Stop it, Maya. We haven't. You haven't. You've always been ready to use this. You're smarter than I am… always have been. All those years I was making weapons, you were working on this. Getting it right, while I was just a guy in an Iron Man suit."

Maya punched a sequence of keys, then slowly pushed a hydraulic press, compiling the final live dose of the Extremis serum. She removed the completed cartridge of serum from the compiler and snapped it into a hypodermic jet injector. She inspected it for a moment, held it up over the operating table, then looked at Tony.

"Ready?"

She held the injector to Tony's shoulder and pulled the trigger, releasing the serum into his blood.

"Hold still," said Maya. "Don't squirm."

"I know this seems impossible," said Tony, "but I always wanted to be more than I already am. Sal said something about that. That he'd tried to instill a sense of the future in us both. That was it. Funny: This is the second time I've had to work against the clock for the Iron Man to save my life."

Tony choked, gagged, and spat up blood. Maya

pulled the jet injector back from his body and let it drop to her side, its cartridge empty.

"One last thing," Tony whispered. "Text Mrs. Rennie. Tell her to...cancel my...meetings."

He jerked violently, howling in pain. Black liquid mixed with blood spewed out of his mouth as his back arched involuntarily. With one final spasm, Tony Stark, the invincible Iron Man, collapsed, limp on the operating table.

FOURTEEN

Oh, God.

Tony felt a steady, painful throbbing in his head. His heart palpitated, thudding erratically. His lungs gurgled, and his joints pounded with pain. He saw nothing but blackness all around. *I've lost my sight,* he thought.

Then he realized: He wasn't supposed to be conscious.

"What's happening, Maya?" But words wouldn't come. He couldn't move his mouth. He couldn't move anything at all. He struggled to speak, to tell Maya that something had gone wrong. To say that he felt trapped— bound in a rigid, thick cast, a stiff coating. That Extremis had caused him to feel nothing but continued agony and exhaustion. The process had failed.

"Can you hear me?" He spoke, but he didn't speak. Like in a dream, except he wasn't able to wake up.

A dull, red glow crept into his peripheral vision.

As it brightened, Tony realized it was a light. A reddish light in a dingy room lined with scrap-heap paneling and sheetrock. A makeshift room in a cave of metamorphic stratified rock. He knew this place. He knew the old, simple ceiling fan that rotated, off-balance, overhead, its blades covered in dust. As if it would fall at any moment.

He'd seen this before.

"Can you hear me? Am I alive?" He could speak now. He could move. Ah, but the pain.

"I can hear you, Mr. Stark. You are alive." That voice...a man's voice. Not Maya. Not Futurepharm.

"AAAaaahh!" Tony jerked up, his eyes wide open now. He coughed, reached for a glass of water that wasn't there. Grabbed at the electrodes Maya had placed on his chest, but they weren't there either.

He lay on a filthy cot in a small, poorly lit room. He knew this place. He was back in the mountains of Afghanistan. His hand went straight to his naked chest, to the damp, bloody bandages. This wasn't real. This was Tony's transformation seizing control of his mind, Extremis invading his most private thoughts and memories.

Why can't I wake up?

"Not so much with the noise, Mister Stark." A warm hand was on his shoulder. Not Maya's small hand, soft from years of desk jobs. The rough hand of a man.

"And not so much with the moving. There is a piece of shrapnel lodged next to your heart. I could not remove it."

Ho Yinsen stood above him. His friend. His savior. The thin, white-haired Asian man who had saved Tony's life after the Stark Sentinel should have killed him.

"I know you." Tony turned his head slightly, furrowed his brow, and spoke the same words he had that day in Kunar province. "We met at a conference in Bern...you're Ho Yinsen, the medical futurist."

"Good memory for one who was so blisteringly drunk," said Yinsen. "If I had been that drunk, I wouldn't have been able to stand, much less give a lecture." He laughed a bit, showing his brown teeth. "I got too used to the easy living of the conference-touring scientist. The hotels. The room service. The expense account. Then you take one wrong turn in a foreign city, and...here I am." He smiled and wrinkled his eyes behind his round, wire-rimmed eyeglasses. He still wore a wrinkled suit, the tie long since removed. His white shirt was unbuttoned casually at the top, stained with blood from some unknown medical emergency. Maybe Tony's own.

"And where's here?"

"A remote camp of the...well, what do we call them? Insurgents? Gunmen? Terrorists? Guerrillas? It is all the same."

Tony leaned forward on the cot.

"They have Yinsen, the great medical innovator, for combat medicine. And now they have Anthony Stark, the great weaponeer. You see this?" Yinsen motioned to a pile of electronics—old CRT monitors, used PCs, worthless mobile phones, cables, unarmed ordnance, makeshift explosives, fuses, broken detonators—stacked on an old door set up as a makeshift table on two sawhorses. "This is your future now. This will shortly be explained to you, probably with great violence."

Tony stared quizzically.

"They want you to build them a weapon that they can use against the Americans," said Yinsen.

"From this?" Tony sat up now, one hand to his chest. "Oh, God, that hurts…"

Yinsen stood up, laughed sharply, and leaned forward. "Lucky for you, your wound is fatal. You will be dead within a week. The shrapnel is moving. You will be slowly stabbed to death by a chunk of your own munitions."

"Swell," said Tony.

"Yinsen is not so lucky. For he is tougher than John Wayne's old boots, and he will live forever."

That sounded like a slight exaggeration, but Tony let it go. "I can't give these people a weapon," he said.

"If you try hard," said Yinsen, mock-cheerfully, "you could make yourself die first."

"You're not helping." Tony scratched his head. That hurt, too. Everything hurt. Getting hit by your own land mine sucked.

"You are lucky to have me as a friend, whitey," said Yinsen.

"Yes, I am," Tony acknowledged. He cracked his neck and began, unsteadily, to push himself to his feet. "In Bern, you were talking about helping land-mine victims in Korea. Magnetic wound excision."

"I cannot remove the shrapnel," said Yinsen, apologetically. "It presses on your heart. There could be a rupture."

"Not remove it," said Tony. "Hold it. Hold it in place. Stop it from working itself in deeper." He stood up.

"AAKKKK!" Tony's heart pounded, and his muscles seized up. He clutched his aching chest and vomited blood. He fell to his knees, spitting more blood on the dirt floor.

"Back to bed with you," said Yinsen. "Die in relative comfort, at least."

Tony crouched on all fours now, unable to stand. He was glad to be still wearing his trousers, the same ones he'd had on when he'd arrived in Kunar. "Did… did you see my presentation at the conference?"

"I am afraid I walked out. Something about exoskeletons for soldiers. War stuff."

"It wasn't for war," Tony gasped, still staring at the floor. "That was just to get the funding. You can't just… *wish* the future into being. I'm a *pragmatic* dreamer. It has to be bought and paid for. Even the munitions I made…were just stealing money from the Army for the real work."

Yinsen was interested now. "And what is the real work?"

"Test-piloting the future. The Iron Man program I floated at the conference is not about exoskeletons or war. It's about becoming better. It's about bringing on the future. The earliest stages of adapting *machine* to *man* and making us great." Tony stood up now. Slouching to stop his chest from aching, he gingerly stepped over to the table of obsolete electronics. He wiped the blood from his mouth.

"We're going to make a prototype Iron Man out of this junk." Tony thought back—forward?—to the present for a moment. To the armor destroyed during the battle on the interstate, now crumpled and lying in a corner of Maya's lab. To his new alloy suit in the briefcase, waiting for him. "A wearable weapon for hosts. And you're going to build a magnetic field generator into the chest plate." He glanced back at Yinsen. "We're going to build something that keeps me alive long enough to get us both out of here. Because my work isn't finished yet."

A mild static shock coursed through Tony's limbs, jolting him back to the present. Extremis was affecting his muscles, flowing through his body and creating localized micro-spasms, but he couldn't move to relieve them. He was held in place, incapacitated by what felt, ironically, like a rigid suit of iron.

Then Maya spoke in a distant, muffled voice.

"Tony? Tony, are you okay in there? You're inside a cocoon of synthesized organic bio-metal. I'm shooting x-rays of your right hand and knee once an hour. I'm seeing progress in the bone structure. The second hour showed all bones in your hand had been rebuilt, and now the knee is being modified. But I can't see anything else because of the cocoon. I thought I'd still get your vital signs through the framework, but they're blocked. I don't know if you're alive. Give me a sign, anything. Try to breathe loudly or something. Whine, moan, anything.

"Tony, can you hear me? Damn you for trying this. This isn't how it was supposed to be."

He tried to respond, tried to see, to open his mouth to ask how exactly she'd thought things *were* supposed to be. But instead he passed out again, losing himself in the past.

Days had gone by now. Tony stood, still shirtless but now with a crude flexible metal plate affixed to his chest. That was Yinsen's magnet, designed to pull the shrapnel away even as it fought to reach Tony's heart.

Tony shielded his eyes from the single generator-powered lamp overhead that lit the musty room. He gave a quick glance at the surveillance camera in the corner and hoped no one was watching. They had to hurry.

"I tell you...either it's finished or I am." He tossed a wrench down on the table.

"It is done...and probably so are you," said Yinsen. He picked up the gray steel chest plate that he and Tony had hammered into shape, and advanced toward Tony. "Quickly now."

Tony slipped his arms through the straps that

would hold the chest plate in place. "Oh, God. That's heavy." Yinsen gave the chest plate a push, adjusting it.

"Will you be able to move?"

"Once the power's on. If the power cells are good, if they're storing and recycling the arc-reactor energy. If my math was right with the palladium we pulled out of that dud warhead. And my math is always right."

Yinsen walked around to tighten the straps across Tony's back.

"Lock it in place, Yinsen. Quickly. It's making my chest tighten."

"It is all I can do to lift it. Hold on a few moments more."

Tony stumbled. "Too heavy."

"Get the power on," said Yinsen.

Tony twisted the rotary switch around the arc reactor on the chest. Later, this would be the technology he'd implant internally, replacing the magnet and keeping the shrapnel at bay. But now, nothing happened. Yinsen went to his bag and dug around.

"The last of my medical kit. A stimulant," he said.

"I have a piece of metal rubbing against my heart… and you want to make it beat *faster*…?"

"Get the power on, Tony."

"I'm trying."

The chest plate sprang to life, glowing white from the palladium arc reactor, and Tony stumbled back in surprise. But he no longer had problems with the weight of the armor.

Yinsen came over with an injector. He pressed it against Tony's neck and depressed the trigger.

"This either saves you or kills you," said Yinsen.

"Either way: Thank you for trying, my friend." Tony glanced up at the security camera. Their captors would be along any minute. "Been a hell of a week, hasn't it? The next bit's going to be really interesting. Let's finish getting this suit on me."

"Wake up, Mr. Stark! This laziness is unacceptable. You have a business to run."

Mrs. Rennie? Tony struggled to open his eyes inside the high-tech cocoon. He couldn't do it.

"The board demands you respond immediately regarding your extended field test of the new phone. Mister America from the Avengers has called several times—something about a fight he saw on the television news—and he seems quite concerned that perhaps you've expired. And your fans weren't happy with the Wonder Wheel, which isn't surprising given what a disaster that excursion was. They want to see your Iron Man creature do tricks for them. And where is your worthless self? Answer me immediately, Mr. Stark, or I shall be forced to inform Ms. Potts that you are with this Maya character, that you replaced your hands with duck noses, and have gone missing."

No, no, thought Tony. *Don't tell Pepper. She won't trust me again. I need her to trust me. She's what is truly good in my life. And she needs to finish her field research… it's crucial to the company's future.*

But Tony couldn't speak, and he had to be imagining this anyway. Mrs. Rennie was in Coney Island. He was in Texas. There's no way she could be here, on the other side of the bio-metallic cocoon, barking demands at him. Would Maya have even let her into the lab? And what was that about duck noses?

Then he realized she wasn't in the room. She was inside the cocoon with him, a big floating Mrs. Rennie head.

"Mister Stark, call me the second you grow your hands back, or use that eye thing you do to tell your fancy phone to call me. How can I expect to run a business with you eating all the toner and sending me all these poodles?"

He hadn't expected a vivid imagination to be a side effect of Extremis. This was worse than that time he and his buddy Rhodey, from the Air Force, had gone to central Africa to negotiate with those warlords who'd claimed to have salvaged warheads. They'd both taken that experimental malaria medication for the CDC trials and started hallucinating. Rhodey had been about to hit him with a rock that was really a hyena, and Tony had been convinced that he was there as a missionary charged with saving Rhodey's soul. Thankfully, a bigger threat—an angry renegade bull elephant—had snapped them out of their delirium.

Stay calm, Tony reminded himself. *Rest. Wait for Extremis to rebuild the body's healing center. Recompile.*

But then Mrs. Rennie morphed into Obadiah Stane's big, bald head, hovering in front of Tony.

"I know where Pepper is, Tony. I'm going to go find her. And when I do, I'm going to force her to tell me what mission you sent her on. She's helpless without Iron Man's protection. And I'll use that information to take over Stark Enterprises—again. Do you remember that, Tony? When your company was mine and not yours? Do you remember how you ended up locked out, living on the streets? How I renamed it Stane International?"

How could Tony possibly forget when his father's business partner had launched a hostile takeover? When he'd used not only legal channels to shut Tony out of his own company, but had also made his own armor and called himself Iron Monger?

How do I change the channel in this hallucination?

"Pepper Potts is anything but helpless, Stane, whether Iron Man's around or not." Tony forced his dream self to argue Pepper's defense. If he stopped trying to move his mouth and accepted that this wasn't real, he could do it. "She's the most competent person I've ever met. She runs circles around you when it comes to business. If Pepper had been trying a hostile takeover against me instead of your pathetic self, Stane, I'd never have gotten back control of the company. I'd still be out on the streets today, drinking myself into a stupor."

"You'll lose her in the end, Stark," said the big, floating Obadiah head. "You don't have what it takes to keep a smart, capable woman interested. You only get the trophies, the pretty ones after your money."

"How can I lose her, you idiot?" said Tony. "I don't

even have her. She still avoids me whenever I try to talk about anything personal."

"You haven't even noticed that Happy Hogan is competing with you. Your own chauffeur, one of your best friends, is trying to steal your girlfriend."

"God, shut up! You don't exist, Stane, and Pepper doesn't need me—or any man—to take care of her. You're a side effect of the Extremis, my own insecurities battling it out in my imagination. If I'd known I'd have to talk to you again, I'd have stuck with dying inside my armor."

"You need some whisky, Stark. It'll help you handle your miserable failure against Mallen. You couldn't protect those innocents driving those cars. Their deaths are your responsibility."

"You just blew it, Stane. Yes, their deaths are my responsibility. But here's why you can't use that against me. Thousands of deaths in war-torn countries around the world have been my responsibility. Small children picking up firewood. Women going to fetch water. Innocents in the line of fire, stumbling over land mines. I *already* can't look at myself in the mirror. You can't drive me to drink because I already live part-time in Hell, right here in my head where you're paying me a visit. You can't scare me any more than I scare myself."

Stane's head fizzled and disappeared.

"Oh, and Stane," Tony called after him. "Iron Monger is a stupid name. And my dad thought you were a jerk."

He willed himself to fall back asleep, to exist in the suspended state between awareness and dreamland, but

Extremis wouldn't cooperate. Extremis was still focused on the evolution of Iron Man.

His origin continued to play out in his head.

In Tony's dream-haze, his chest glowed from the arc reactor. He fired a blast at the door that had been keeping Yinsen and himself imprisoned. Yinsen fell back as Tony—clumsy in the armor he'd built—stumbled, then dragged his steel-and-iron-covered frame through the door. He emerged into the tunnels that honeycombed these caves, deep in the Afghan mountains.

Insurgents with guns—men in camouflage and combat boots, with their heads covered against the sand and sun outside the caves—poured into the dark tunnel, racing toward the huge gray creature that Tony had transformed into.

He stood for a moment, glowing from his arc reactor—towering, invulnerable, and powerful in his steel shell.

Five men turned and fired their assault rifles at Iron Man. Tony shielded his eyes—which, in the first armor, had been exposed behind slits—with the metal gauntlet on his left forearm. The bullets pounded his armor, but did not break through.

"You people wanted Stark micro-munitions?" he asked. "Have some."

Iron Man stretched out his right arm toward the insurgents and fired a quick barrage of pellets cannibalized from a defunct seedpod, one from each finger. They exploded at the terrorists' feet, engulfing the men in an explosive blast of flame.

Tony heard bullets pinging off his back, not unlike the sound of heavy rain echoing on a corrugated metal roof. More men were running at him, attacking from behind ammunition-storage sheds, firing machine guns and rifles. He spotted the muzzle flashes and turned around slowly—the first Iron Man armor hadn't been very nimble—and aimed a hand at the men. He depressed a switch inside his palm guard. There had been no artificial intelligence in the first armor, either. Everything had been manually controlled.

A repulsor beam blasted the men, knocking them aside and leaving them lifeless on the rocky ground. Tony clicked a lever in his left glove, igniting a spark. Flames shot from his outstretched hand, incinerating the ammunition sheds and everyone he saw on his way out of the cave. He could smell the burning bodies.

Another bonus of his modern armor: It was airtight.

And then there was daylight. He breathed the outside air and gazed at the sky. How long had it been?

Tony heard an engine and the squeal of brakes. He turned to see a Jeep pulling around a building, screeching to a halt, its passenger aiming an Uzi right at him. Tony wanted to fly away, but he hadn't yet invented boot jets.

BLAM BLAM BLAM. Tony was struck three times right in the chest. He glanced down to see small dents where he'd been hit. *This armor is tough,* he thought.

He raised his head slowly, angrily, and his arc reactor glowed.

"Weapons test," said Iron Man. A fiery uni-beam blast shot out of his chest, annihilating the Jeep.

And then there was only fire, thick black smoke, explosions, and the foul stench of burning diesel.

Iron Man stood triumphantly among the flames.

FIFTEEN

"Aaaah!" Maya yelped with surprise as Tony's chest repulsor blasted through, lasering away his rigid Extremis cocoon-shell.

Tony had regained consciousness a moment ago, and found himself still unable to move. *Enough of this,* he'd thought. *Get this bio-metal off me.* No more restraint—Mallen had too much of a headstart on Iron Man. Tony didn't have time for Extremis to finish processing, to naturally dissolve its husk.

So, with a single thought, Tony sent out a network of Extremis-powered mini-bursts throughout the cocoon. The electromagnetic bursts followed his neural path network, sizzling red below the hard cover and burning it away.

The bio-metal evaporated and fell to the floor as if it

had been shed. Tony lay naked on the operating table, the lab around him dark aside from the blue lights of the computer monitors and the white glow from his chest. He sent one more thought-command out through his system.

Remove electrodes and IV. The connectors and tubes snapped off him, sparking as they dissolved.

"I'm alive," said Tony. "I'll be damned." He lay still for a moment, marveling that all the pain he'd felt was gone, the delirium had vanished. He felt fantastic, alive, alert, ready to arm-wrestle Captain America and the Hulk at the same time, one with each arm, while simultaneously rescuing Pepper from an alien invasion.

"Tony, don't try to move!" Maya stood over him, a panicked, high-pitched edge to her voice. She held out her hand to stop him.

"I am so sick of people saying that to me," said Tony. He sat up. "How long was I out?"

"Twenty-four hours. This is way too fast."

Maya was checking Tony's vitals and pulling up his eyelids, looking to see whether all was normal. "I made a few alterations to your compiling program while you were out of the room," he said. "Removed some safeties. Ow, stop poking me."

"You did what?" She stood back, stunned.

"Improved your work, Maya. When I said you were smarter than me? I was just trying to make you feel more confident. You seemed nervous, you know? So, what—were you just staring at me for 24 hours? Take a nice long look? When did I lose my circuit-skin?"

"You still had your underwear on when the cocoon grew, if that's what you're wondering," said Maya, averting her eyes as Tony stood up. "You must have burned it off yourself, show-off. And there's nothing new to see here, so don't flatter yourself. Whatever you grew must be on the inside." She smirked.

"And I didn't just stare at you, for your information. I was busy playing with this amazing device." She waved Tony's phone. "I watched *Billionaire Boys and Their Toys* and kept an eye on your messages in case you got something important from Nick Fury or the president. Who's Pepper?"

"Why, did she text?"

"Only fourteen times."

"Not so loud," Tony winced. "I think I've grown new ear tissue." He held out his newly repaired right hand and examined it. He clenched and unclenched his fist. "How about that? Brand new. Hey, that looks like what I'd plug my stereo speakers into when I was a kid." He'd noticed a port in his forearm. He glanced down at his chest to find additional ports all over his body.

"Let's see if the other stuff I grew works," he said. "*Start.*" Tony felt a mild humming sensation in his muscles and realized: *I'm online.*

"These things are on your back, too, and they're symmetrical," said Maya, her scientific curiosity overcoming her modesty. She examined one closely. "Tony...this wasn't part of Extremis before. What have you done?"

Tony smiled a toothy grin. The humming had

subsided; he was no longer tired or delirious. He really felt spectacularly well.

"This," he said. The port on his shoulder blade turned golden. It grew and multiplied, transforming into a web of copper-colored biometal that honeycombed across his skin, spreading quickly over his entire body to cover him in a conductive subskin layer that was part of his actual anatomy. It moved up his body within moments, blanketing his neck and skull, leaving only his face exposed.

"Supercompressed and stored in the hollows of my bones, Maya. I carry the crucial undersheath of the Iron Man suit inside my body now. That's why I won't be needing to wear it or carry it around. That's why Extremis dissolved the sheath I used to wear."

He turned and faced her. "It's wired directly into my brain. I control the Iron Man with my thoughts now. Like it was another limb."

He glanced across the room at the case that held his armor.

"Look, watch the briefcase that Mrs. Rennie sent me."

The briefcase popped open with a thought. Tony didn't even need to touch it to reveal the parts of the Iron Man armor within.

"How did you do that?" Maya was astonished.

"I sent the signal from the lockchip in my arm."

Maya's phone buzzed, and she glanced at it. "Oh, Hell. Don't do anything for a second," she said. "I have to take this…"

She put the phone up to her ear, keeping an eye on Tony as she did so. "Maya Hansen."

"Hello, Maya. It's Tony." She held the phone a few inches away and stared at it as the voice continued. "Note carefully how my lips are not moving, and that there's nothing up my sleeve. If you like, I could do this while drinking a glass of water."

"Stop it, Tony! You are freaking me out," yelled Maya. She threw the phone at him. He ducked easily, and it hit the wall behind him, then clattered to the floor.

"Don't watch this next bit, then," Tony said, laughing. He raised his arms dramatically.

The Iron Man suit, section by section, rose up out of the case as if by magic. The pieces levitated and moved toward Tony through the air, seemingly propelled only by thought. They attached themselves to him, each section placing itself carefully where it was intended to go, then clicking into place. The shin guards clung to his shins. The chest guard covered his chest. The helmet enveloped his skull and face, and clicked together with no visible seam.

"How are you doing that?" Maya was a scientist. She didn't believe in magic, but she was stumped.

"Vectored repulsor field." Tony was casual in his response. "Just lightly pushing stuff from different angles."

Fully assembled now in familiar red-and-gold armor, Tony stepped forward into the light, clenched the fist on his rebuilt right hand, and struck a proud pose.

The new Iron Man suit was sleeker and more stylish than the one destroyed in the battle with Mallen. The slotted eyes glowed an eerie white against the smooth golden mask. The arc reactor shone through the alloy chest plate in a pale-yellow triangle. He flipped the visor on his helmet up and down with a thought, testing an extension of his body that now felt as natural as his own arms and legs.

"I am Iron Man," said Tony. "Inside and out."

"My God." Maya stood in front of the results of her collaboration with Tony Stark, small next to the Iron Man armor. She reached out a hand, brushing the arc reactor faintly with the tips of her fingers, almost caressing this physical manifestation of her years of dogged research. "We have to run some tests. Remember Sal's warning about emergent-tech tendencies, Tony. You'll still be evolving in the near future. You can't anticipate the changes you'll go through! That's dangerous. And the strain on your internal organs…"

"Grew new ones." Iron Man turned away and walked out the lab door. "I need to go to work. Mallen's still out there, and he's a day closer to Washington, D.C., now."

Maya chased along behind him. "We don't know exactly where he is."

Iron Man stopped, turned, and stared at her. "Maya, I can see through satellites now."

He turned and strode away, alone, down the darkened hallway.

SIXTEEN

Mallen heard the mountain man, blowing the harp in an old stone quarry, long before he saw him.

Mallen was hiking through a forest, somewhere in Virginia. There wasn't too much farther to go, he knew, before he got to the suburbs of Washington, D.C. He'd seen signs along the eastbound highway a few hours back when he'd emerged from a protected mountain valley at Front Royal. He'd veered away from the interstate and even the back roads to avoid altercations. Not that the authorities had a chance against Mallen's new powers, but he didn't feel like fighting all the way to the United States' capital city.

The harmonica echoed through the forest of old oak and hickory trees. Whoever was playing it was extraordinary, creating train sounds and mimicking whooping and hooting. Mallen was no music or blues aficionado, but he knew this was exceptional.

He followed the sound of the music down a ridge from a dirt road. But it stopped when he got closer, and the sound of howling dogs filled the air.

Mallen ran closer, leaping over boulders as he rushed down a slope to arrive at the edge of a small quarry. A wiry old mountain man covered in whiskers stood above the quarry on a small Caterpillar bulldozer. He held a harmonica in one hand and a half-full unmarked bottle of clear liquid in the other.

"Shaddup, Bob! Blue, sit down! That bear ain't gonna hurt you. Shut the hell up. I was playin' the harp up here."

A black-and-tan coon dog and a bluetick hound were braying at a medium-sized black bear that had been unlucky enough to stumble on to the scene. The dogs had cornered the bear up against the rock wall of the stone quarry.

"You need some help here, mister?" Mallen leapt down into the quarry and strode past the dogs. He grabbed the bear's midsection with his hands and, holding it upside-down, lifted it above his head.

"Down, boys!" the mountain man hollered at his dogs. They kept howling and jumping at Mallen. The bear wriggled its legs furiously.

Mallen pitched the bear, feet first, up over the quarry and into the woods. The dogs set off, chasing the bear as if it were a stick, howling all the way.

"Thank you kindly, sir," said the mountain man.

"Though it ain't bear season right now."

"Well, I don't see a game warden around, Mister, uh…"

"Lee Jefferson Davis Tecumseh Sherman, but you can call me Slim."

"All right, Slim. This your place?"

"Hell no, boy. This here's my quarry. My place is up yonder." Slim motioned up the mountain. "You wanna drink?" He held out the unmarked bottle.

"Sure." Mallen took a swig of the liquid. It tasted fiery and gross. He spat it out on the leaves, accidentally breathing sparks and starting a small fire.

"Sorry," said Mallen. He stamped out the fire.

Slim laughed. "My moonshine ain't never done that before. What brings you 'round here, stranger?"

"I'm from Texas, on my way to have a talk with the government. I'm going to set things straight."

"Good for you, boy," said Slim. "I stood up to the Feds, too. They wanted to take this mountain for a national park. I said fine, you can make all the parks you want, but this is my quarry and my land, and you can't take it cuz my wife and I been living here thirty years and this is how I make money. So y'all make your Bull Run National Park around my land, and I'll be in a little island in the middle, but I want y'all to blaze my land as private property to keep out trespassers when they come hiking nearby. Cuz otherwise, I might shoot 'em or my dogs might eat 'em."

"So you stopped them?"

"I sure as hell did. I went down to community

meetings, and I wrote letters to the editor. I played the harp through my nose, and I sang my ballad, and I clogged for the rich neighbors at the meetings, and they said this here's a real mountain man, let's help old Slim here hang on to his home. Of course, they like their land, too, but they can't clog, so they had to do it with city lawyers."

"Whatever works," Mallen agreed. "Me, I got something a little more direct in mind. You see what I did with the fire? I have this stuff in me, makes me stronger than everyone. Got it from a lab guy down in Texas. He was in the bar downtown, a few stools away from me and my buds, and he was tryin' to be cool. 'Hey, bartender,' he said, 'here's ten bucks.' Then he winks at the guy, like he's Ginger on Gilligan's Island, like he's a girl, and asks if any of his customers might have a bug up his butt about the government or military. Bartender told him to go to hell and still kept his ten bucks."

Mallen laughed now, and Slim laughed, too.

"We went and talked to the guy then. Got something from him, an injection. Stick it right in the base of the skull, he told me and my friends. That's the nerve center. It'll make you stronger. Well, it did. I'm a walking weapon. I can make my point, and they have to listen."

"You're a regular freedom fighter then, boy," said Slim with a chuckle. "Come on up the hill. My wife will have coffee brewin', and then I got something to show you, freedom fighter."

"What's that?"

Slim slid down off the bulldozer and started walking up the hill. Mallen followed him.

"I found some ruins in the hills. I found some artifacts. I think it was a fort from Mosby's Rangers."

"Who?"

Slim stopped and stared at Mallen.

"Boy, if you weren't from Texas, I'd clobber you right now. You're walking through the front lines of the Civil War. Right where we're standing, didn't you know this land changed hands more than thirty times?"

Mallen looked blankly at Slim. He came from an entirely different part of the country and hadn't paid much attention during history class. Plus, he'd dropped out as soon as he legally could.

"Mosby was a freedom fighter—the gray ghost of the Confederacy. A colonel," explained Slim, with exasperation. "His rangers rode through these hills, harassing the other side. He was what you wish you were, and he did it without breathing fire, with just regular manpower. Come on—I'll show you."

The dogs—Bob and Blue—came running back and escorted the two men as they picked their way over the boulders up the slope to the dirt road. Mallen marveled that Slim could make out the trail. Even with his Extremis-enhanced eyesight, he could barely see it.

The men crossed the road and climbed a rocky driveway, passing old pickup trucks and doghouses.

"I sleep there when the wife throws me out," said Slim, pointing to an old truck.

"Looks like you use it for target practice, too," said Mallen. The truck was covered in bullet holes. Slim reminded Mallen of his dad. He'd have to stop back by here after his business in Washington, find out how Slim knew so much about the Civil War. Maybe he could help Slim with the quarry, now that he was so strong. Be nice to help good Americans do concrete, useful stuff.

"Yeah, I set up bottles there and shoot. That's why I drink all the time," said Slim. "I need the bottles."

"C'mon, Blue." Slim stopped at the top of the hill, outside a trailer. He fastened Blue to a chain outside a doghouse and walked Bob over to another little house. Slim headed to a pump in the yard, pumped the handle a few times to fill up a bucket with water, then walked to both doghouses to fill up the water bowls. The dogs both flopped down, exhausted from their outing.

Smoke rose up from a chimney pipe in the corner of the trailer. "Let's go in and have some coffee," said Slim. "Then we'll go look at Mosby's fort."

They climbed the few stairs to the dusty old trailer. An old black man with glasses sat in a rocking chair next to a woodstove, watching television.

"Hey, Popcorn! You got lunch ready? I have a guest." Slim turned to Mallen. "My wife's name is Sonny, but I call him Popcorn. Been callin' him Popcorn for three decades, not gonna stop now just because it annoys him."

"Him?" Mallen stood, shocked amid the dust of the little trailer.

"Yeah, my wife's a he! Don't tell me you're one of them city slickers with some kinda strict ideas about how life is. Nothin' ain't ever like you think it's supposed to be. You gotta live your own way. Gotta follow your heart."

"Slim," Popcorn said, "what the hell were the dogs chasing? I heard them barking all the way up here."

Mallen stared at Slim and Popcorn now, uncertain how to react. Part of him wanted to bash Slim's brains out, then burn up the whole trailer with Popcorn inside of it. But instead, he mumbled to Slim that he didn't care all that much for Mosby.

"I gotta go," said Mallen. "Nice to meet you. I got a meeting with the president."

He turned and hurried away. But as he went, he heard Slim hollering after him.

"Read up on Mosby, boy! Joined the Feds after the war—knew when to stop. You could learn a thing or two from him."

Slim went back to playing his harmonica. The joyful sound of the harp followed Mallen like a ghost, all the way down the mountain, as he made his way toward the state road through the valley.

SEVENTEEN

Iron Man flew high over Texas, Arkansas, and Tennessee, his gold-and-red armor gleaming in the bright morning sunlight. He had just passed Cumberland Gap—where Tennessee, Kentucky, and Virginia meet—and zoomed over the mountains and gorges that looked like a green spine from the air. Geological and agricultural information flashed across his HUD as he glanced at the landscape below.

He was on his way to Washington, D.C., hunting for Mallen. His newly enhanced armor allowed him to scan through thousands of law-enforcement databases, much faster than before. Images flickered before him, almost at the speed of thought.

But his mind kept wandering to the scenery. He remembered meeting a couple of women, once, who'd said they were going to hike the Appalachian Trail. *Maybe I'll try that one day…see if Rhodey or Pepper wants to come along. But with my luck, I'd wind up alone at 5,000 feet with Mrs. Rennie.*

Mallen's name popped up on some search results. Tony used his optical systems to click each entry open, read it, then click the next.

"Let's see…Mallen," Tony read aloud. "No first name? Okay, Mallen it is. Parents were killed twenty years ago in a shootout with the FBI after his father shot a federal agent. Shuttled from foster home to foster home, primarily a ward of the state of Texas. Described as bitter, erratic, racist views, low I.Q., no known intimate relationships. Well, that's not exactly a shock."

He scanned down. "Frequent legal trouble, extremist beliefs, probable substance-abuser, several weapons arrests, no convictions. Many low-end service jobs, none long-term. And a poor dresser, too, based on the one time we met. He's a charmer."

Jarvis suddenly broke off the data stream.

"Multiple small mammals are approaching," said Jarvis.

"What? Flying monkeys? We're fifty feet in the air. Could you be a bit more speci…"

Then Tony was engulfed in a swarm of squeaking blackness.

"Gah! What the…?" Tony dodged and weaved rapidly, but the tiny, flying animals were all around him. He lurched and veered, surprised at his own incredible speed. He was totally surrounded, and the only light he saw came from his boot jets. "Bats! Jarvis, identify species."

"These are little brown bats, Mister Stark."

"I can see that, genius. Maybe you need an Extremis upgrade, too."

"I have access to thousands of databases via my Zipsat due to your upgrade, sir. These are *Myotis lucifugus*. One of the most common bats in North America." Jarvis displayed a Fish and Wildlife Service file.

"Oh, I see," said Tony. "Little brown bat really is its name. I, uh, knew that. Scan article for description of diurnal activities."

"Daytime activities include sleeping and grooming."

"My kind of people."

The creatures continued to surround him, flapping and screeching. Why was he surrounded by flying bats during daylight hours? Suddenly, he remembered that his hearing had improved. What would the bats sound like to his Extremis-enhanced ears? "Jarvis, give me frequency scaling."

He slowed to a hover now and listened. Tony had made his first bat detector in second grade, so he was curious about the audible difference between his science project and his own newly improved ears. He heard a deep rumbling in the distance—but between dodging bats and listening to the remarkable spectrum of their chirps, he didn't give much thought to the distant noise.

"Switch on echolocation. Let's see if I can fly like them, too, without visuals."

Iron Man listened to the bat squeaks, fascinated. He glanced at the volume control on his HUD and turned it up. Then a little more. Then more.

WHOOOOM! A thunderous boom startled Tony. He fell to the ground, still blind, landing flat on his face.

The rumbling. He'd been so busy with the bats, he hadn't investigated it.

"Two persons are nearby," stated Jarvis, flatly.

"Ugh. You can lower the volume a bit," said Tony.

Iron Man rolled over and sat up. Above him, the pack of bats dissipated, flapping away. He glanced around. He'd fallen into a small limestone gorge. He spotted a craggy overhang that had doubtlessly been home to the bats.

Then he noticed: Just below the rugged overhang, two hikers stood frozen in fear. The rocky cliff above them shuddered, rumbling louder now. Threatening a rockslide.

In a flash, Iron Man fired up his jet boots and zoomed toward the hikers, maneuvering swiftly through the gorge. He'd grab them both and have them out of the way before the rock gave way.

Since he'd become Iron Man, Tony had trained himself to head straight into danger—to run *toward* fear rather than away from it. Extremis had made him all the faster. Tony marveled at his own speed and precision.

Then he overshot, smashing right into the cliff face at a hundred miles an hour. The impact jarred his helmet, dazing him. He shook his head, dislodging himself from the rock.

Looks like your serum is a little too *powerful, Maya.*

Then, to Tony's horror, the cliff around him collapsed. Rocks, roots and dirt hailed down all around him.

"Run!" he yelled.

My fault, he thought. *Again.*

One of the hikers, a young blond man in a "Virginia is for Lovers" baseball cap, hesitated; the other, a college-age woman in a red T-shirt, started to run. She moved left, then right, but rocks were crashing down all around her. She covered her head and knelt.

"This area was once a vast inland sea," said Jarvis. He was still receiving information from local and national databases.

"*What?* Repulsors, now!" Iron Man backed up against the remains of the cliff, anchoring himself as best he could. He stretched out his arms and sprayed a volley of bright, focused micro-bursts, hundreds of them flashing across the landscape like a light show at a heavy-metal concert. Each repulsor burst precisely targeted a single piece of rock or debris, exploding it with the force of a stick of dynamite.

A light mist of dust settled on top of the hikers.

Huh. Tony looked at his palms, considering his new, pinpoint repulsor control. He'd been able to produce the precise barrage of micro-bursts with just a thought. *Lesson number one: Learn to use your tools. Lesson number two: And what a set of tools they are.*

Another low rumble came from above, reminding Tony of the emergency at hand.

He jetted down to the hikers.

"Let's go," he said, grabbing one under each arm. He lifted them up, rose above the trees, and slowly flew half a mile east. He landed cautiously alongside a trail, gently releasing his two passengers.

They looked both dazed and relieved. "Crikey," said the female hiker. "That was fun. What's next?"

"Australian, huh?" Tony hadn't realized the hikers were foreign tourists.

"Yeah, we're from northern New South Wales, near the border of Queensland," said the young man. "It's green, like here. Have you been, Iron Bloke?"

Jarvis cut in again. "Augusta County sheriff's department radioed in a Mallen sighting to the state police yesterday afternoon. He bought coffee at a gas station, and a local recognized him from the newspaper. Confirmed by surveillance-camera footage."

"Let's see it."

Jarvis located the police video and streamed it to Tony.

"Yep, that's our man. Any more?"

"Additional sighting: a 7-11 in Prince William County."

"He's almost to Washington," said Tony, suddenly worried. "I have to go."

He rocketed into the air without even saying goodbye.

On the ground, the couple watched him go. "Take it easy, Iron Bloke," the Australian man called out.

EIGHTEEN

The morning sunlight shone in through the window of the campground cabin. Mallen had broken into the cabin at midnight. Now he rolled over on the double bed and sat up.

He flexed his arms a few times, marveling at the strength and stamina he'd had the last few days. Running from Texas to Virginia had been less exhausting than walking a football field had been last month. He wished the camping cabins came with bedding and indoor plumbing, but this had been a decent place to spend the night. *And free, if breaking locks is no problem for you,* he thought.

The bathhouse was a short walk away, so Mallen got up to have as routine a morning as he'd had all week. He headed over to the men's side of the bathhouse and went into one of the shower stalls, to stand under the deliciously warm water for five minutes. All his senses had been improved, and the shower echoed in his ears as a steady stream of water pounded the tile. He smelled the chlorine in the water, heard the shower next to his, could hear from the tone of the water when the man in the next stall soaped up or rinsed off. He also heard the man breathing loudly—he was slightly over-weight. Mallen could sense so many things now.

He felt newly energized. He was ready for today's mission, ready to fix the country. Men with badges were insignificant and had no right to try to control him. Soon, they'd understand that. The world would be back on track.

Dripping wet and naked, Mallen looked for a towel. There wasn't one, so he shook off like a dog, picked up his dirty clothes, and left the stall. An old beach towel hung over the door next to his, so he grabbed it and used it, then threw it in the sink. Some men's clothes hung there, too. The jeans were too big, and the shirt would hang loose on his frame. But at least it didn't smell like it had been worn for three days, the way his own shirt did. *That'll do,* he thought as he pulled it over his head.

"What the hell are you doing?" An unshaven, naked, middle-aged man, flabby and dripping wet, stood outside the shower now, glaring at Mallen. "That's my shirt. My towel. You filthy freak—who do you think you are?"

"Your jeans are too big," said Mallen. "You need to cut back on the all-you-can-eat buffets, man."

The man sputtered in shock as Mallen turned and walked away. He felt the wet towel hit him on the back now, thrown by the angry camper. Mallen turned back slowly to face him.

"I was trying not to cause a fuss," said Mallen. "It's just a towel. A shirt." He reached an arm out, wrapped his hand around the man's thick neck and squeezed.

The camper's eye bulged as Mallen lifted him from the floor.

"You don't know what you're dealing with," said Mallen. "You should be grateful that I need your clothes. I'm a hero, and you're nothing. I'm going to let you go, this time, because you don't understand."

He dropped the man to the floor. As the man gasped for breath, Mallen picked up the jeans and rifled through the pockets. A phone. He tossed that into the sink with a clatter, then turned on the faucet. Didn't need this guy calling the cops. A wallet. He took the wallet and dropped the jeans back to the floor.

"Five bucks. That I can use." Mallen paged past photos and business cards, then came to a work ID.

"What's this?" He studied it, then looked at the naked man, lying before him on the tiles. He stepped closer and used his foot to press the man's head to the floor.

"You work for the government?"

"Just…just a clerk. I'm in maps. I make maps. For the Army."

Mallen stared at the man, gross, slippery, and squirming. The Army. How did Mallen feel about the Army? Was this man a true American or a traitor?

For the second time in two days, Mallen was confused about someone he'd met. He wondered now whether maybe he should have burned the mountain man's trailer.

Oh, to hell with it, he thought. He took his foot off the man's head, lifted him by the throat, and threw him back into the shower stall. The man hit the wall and slumped to the floor, leaving a red trail of blood down the wall.

"Either he lives or dies," said Mallen. "Let God choose." He pulled the shower stall door closed and left the bathhouse.

Mallen stopped at the camp store to pick up a cup of coffee and a corn muffin. He sat down on a bench in front of the store to enjoy his coffee in the morning sun.

He chuckled at yesterday's newspaper on the bench next to him.

TONY STARK FAILS.

It bothered him that the newspaper said Iron Man was still alive. Should have finished him off. *Now he'll be coming after me,* Mallen realized.

"Morning," said a husky voice. Mallen looked up to see a man in a uniform approaching.

Mallen tensed up and slowly placed his coffee and muffin on the ground. He hadn't paid for the cabin or the park entry fee, and he only had the five bucks he'd taken from the guy in the shower. And what about the guy in the shower? Were the rangers already looking for him? Impossible…it would take hours before a cleaner or camper curiously pushed open the stall door. Unless the blood had trickled out into the tile floor.

Fight or talk, he thought. He could easily take this man's head off with a swift blow, but that would make the other campers nervous, and he didn't feel like killing anyone at the moment. He felt like finishing his breakfast.

"Morning, officer."

"What? I'm not—oh, this." The man motioned at his pale-blue wool trousers and hip-length navy-blue jacket. He lifted up a musket Mallen hadn't spotted before. "I'm a reenactor! We're doing a living history event at the Civil War battlefield next door. You wanna come by? I got a spare uniform."

Mallen chuckled. "What, me, a government conscript? No thanks." He picked up his coffee and took a sip. "I've got a little reenacting of my own to do up in Washington, D.C. I'm thinking about playing John Wilkes Booth."

The reenactor looked puzzled, then gave a nervous, uncertain laugh. "Be careful with that role. His big plans didn't do much for him, in the end."

"He died for his country."

"He should've stuck with Shakespeare. I've got to go, or I'll be late attacking Stonewall Jackson." The actor turned away, then stopped for a second and looked back. "If you make it to the battlefield sometime, try the cell-phone tour."

Mallen nodded and finished his coffee. He glanced around at the tall trees that shaded the campground, and the brilliant pink and blue hues of the morning sky. He had about thirty miles to go on this perfect morning. He'd head in across one of the bridges over the Potomac—nice of the Feds to put most of their agencies so close to each other—and sort out this country once and for all. Then he'd get a hot dog and wait to see if that Iron Man loser showed up.

"Evacuation of the area is complete, Iron Man. He's all yours."

"Thank you, director." Iron Man soared above Washington, over the Jefferson Memorial toward the grassy mall that stretched between the Washington Monument and the Capitol. He was lucky Mallen had headed here so early in the morning, before the tourists arrived; but workers would be showing up soon on Capitol Hill. And not just politicians, thought Tony. Support staff, cafeteria workers, librarians, dishwashers, security guards, interns, journalists. Regular people going to earn livings at their jobs. They needed protection.

The lives lost back in Texas weighed heavily on Tony's mind. He'd been overconfident, attacking a psychotic murderer in proximity of the highway. He'd ignored Sal's warnings about potentially being surpassed by more powerful technology, and innocents had paid the price. This time, he needed to wind things up without any bystanders in range. No more deaths would be on his hands.

But now he had brain-linked access to security systems, police records, and public-transportation schedules. He had real-time updates on the surrounding blocks and knew exactly where the bystanders were. This time, Iron Man was ready.

He zoomed in on Mallen with his targeting crosshairs. The Texan was heading up Independence Avenue in the same leather jacket he'd worn when they'd fought on the interstate outside Houston. It was deteriorating, full of rips and tears from Iron Man's bomblet explosions. Mallen swaggered with obvious arrogance, not bothering to conceal himself. As if nothing on Earth could be a threat to him.

"That's a lock, Jarvis," said Tony. "Thrust at 70 percent."

Iron Man flew in lower, just close enough for his repulsor beams to be effective. He stretched out his right arm and pointed his palm at Mallen. A brilliant white circle flashed on Iron Man's gauntlet for a microsecond.

"Fire."

A single candescent repulsor streaked through the morning sky, blasting Mallen directly on the back with the force of a bazooka.

The beam flattened Mallen. He landed face down—the impact cracking and cratering the pavement, the shockwaves upending and crushing two parked cars.

Text flashed across Tony's HUD, identifying the owners of the cars. *Ignore,* thought Tony. *Extraneous information.*

Iron Man closed his fist and aimed directly at Mallen again.

"Seedpods."

Ten spherical bomblets zoomed out of Iron Man's gauntlet. They exploded directly on top of Mallen—on his legs, feet, and back—peppering and battering him with direct hits and shrapnel.

Mallen rolled over and glared at Iron Man. He wasn't hurt, but he'd lost his shredded leather jacket now. He was furious.

Iron Man hovered, his glowing right palm aimed at Mallen like a loaded gun. Smoke and debris blocked out the sun—the only light shone from Iron Man's eyes, armed gauntlet, and jet boots.

"Mister Mallen," Iron Man said. "Lay on the ground. Hands behind your head, ankles crossed."

Mallen leapt to his feet, baring his teeth like a rabid dog. "I've been given a tool to save people like me from criminals in the White House. And I'm going to use it!"

Tony's arc reactor pulsed. He lowered himself to the ground next to one of the wrecked cars.

"You know why you frighten me?" Tony said. "Why I had to deal with you myself?"

Iron Man lifted the wrecked car with one hand. He raised it above his head, his chest reactor burning white. "Flame," said Tony as he took aim at the tires with directional flames. "Repulse," he added. He opened the fuel tank with a repulsive force beam, letting the fuel escape in a cloud of fine droplets. "Laser," he said, finally, igniting the vapor cloud as he hurled the car through the air.

The car struck Mallen and exploded. Mallen stumbled and vanished in a fiery mass of flame and black smoke.

He burned and twisted in the blaze. The stench of fuel and tires was enough to asphyxiate a normal human, or even a super-human.

"I made the first version of this suit to save myself and a friend from criminals with guns. I must've killed fifty people trying to free us. Do you think that was fun for me, killing fifty people?" Iron Man landed on the ground and clenched his fist. *"And my friend still died."*

He advanced on the ball of fire and aimed his fist straight at Mallen's head.

"A stray bullet went through the side of the hut, killed him instantly. And I didn't even know, not for hours. He saved my life, and I fought to protect him, but he was already dead."

Iron Man swung at Mallen with all his might. Mallen shot backward out of the flames and sailed through the air for half a block, crashing through a concrete wall into the Air and Space Museum gift shop.

Mallen leapt to his feet as Iron Man landed in front of him near a glass counter and a bank of cash registers. He stood in front of miniature airplanes and hot air balloons, among T-shirts and inflatable space shuttles.

"My folks died the same way," said Mallen, still steaming from the flames, his clothes shredded and burning. The smell of tires mixed with the stench of astronaut ice cream.

"And you killed fifty people you never met, *twenty years later,*" yelled Tony. He delivered a roundhouse kick to Mallen's face and, at exactly the same moment, let loose a repulsor thrust from his right boot jet. "You're my nightmare: the version of me that couldn't see the future."

Iron Man stood over Mallen now and blasted him with a point-blank repulsor beam.

"You're some murder-happy hillbilly who never in his life had a thought about what these tools are for! It's about responsibility, not killing, the very future in your veins. You don't deserve Extremis," said Tony. *"It's not meant for revenge!"*

Mallen fell back again, crashing through a wall and outside on to the National Mall.

"Shut up!" screamed Mallen, from a pile of rubble and dirt. He stretched his hand out toward Iron Man. His fingertips started to crackle with electrical pulses. Something that looked like a lightning bolt shot out of them.

"I'm not there anymore," said Tony from behind Mallen. Even he was surprised at how fast he was, now that he'd undergone the Extremis process. "I upgraded."

Mallen stared over his shoulder in shock. Tony thought: *Time to end this.* He struck Mallen ferociously across the back, tearing the last of Mallen's shredded shirt from his frame. Mallen fell, lying bare-chested on the grass below Tony.

"I'm as fast as you now, and I can operate this suit by thought," said Iron Man. "I have experience, technology, and a superior dose of Extremis I compiled myself. You don't even know what that means. You've lost the arms race."

Mallen stared up at Iron Man from the ground, his eyes those of a fierce predator.

"I've spent years trying to get out of the arms business, and you forced me back into it," said Tony. "Years trying to turn this suit into something that doesn't just kill.

"Back off and be reasonable. You can still live through this, Mallen. I believe in second chances. Hell, third and fourth chances. Stop looking for revenge and use your gifts to help the world."

"I *am* helping people," said Mallen, glaring.

Mallen opened his mouth and spewed a fireball. The flames engulfed Iron Man's left gauntlet briefly, then sputtered out from the armor's fireproofing. Tony smiled inside the helmet.

"You're slow, Mallen. And clueless."

Roaring, Mallen leapt forward.

"Grid," said Tony. His HUD instantly displayed a digital map of the municipal electric system, with his current location pinpointed by Stark Zipsat GPS and marked in red.

As Mallen crashed down on to Iron Man, Tony pointed his palm at the street below him, blasting a hole in the asphalt with his repulsor beam. He reached into the hole, grabbed a thick insulated electricity cable, and yanked.

Iron Man thrust the live electric main straight into Mallen's chest, copper end first.

Glowing lightning crackled and sparked, electrocuting Mallen. The shock sent him flying backward through the air, crashing through windows and reddish-brown bricks, straight into a museum housing an exhibit on the 1964 World's Fair.

"Oh, God," Mallen whimpered. He lay between an exhibit of electric toothbrushes and a life-size plastic stegosaurus from a display about petroleum products.

And then Iron Man was on top of him, punching again. Tony lifted Mallen by the throat, held him for a second, then threw him through the wall again, back outside.

Tony stood up in the Howard Stark Car of the Future section of the World's Fair exhibit, under a photo of his father meeting some admirers. He hesitated a minute, realizing that the woman shaking his father's hand looked familiar. *Whatever,* thought Tony. *I'll look at that later.* He used his ocular zoom to snap a quick shot of the image, then turned back to using the museum's security system to see where Mallen had gone.

Mallen smacked into the hydraulic boom of a backhoe on a worksite, over on the mall side of the museum. Extremis had again evolved its tech to the situation at hand, and Mallen appeared to be faster and stronger than he'd been in Houston. Back there, he'd been all fists and fire; now he had developed speed and agility.

Mallen grabbed on to the chain hoist that hung from the boom of the backhoe. He leapt up, swinging through the air with ease, then landed upright next to the backhoe. He yanked at the chain, tearing it from the boom, and began swinging the chain's sling hook in steady, menacing circles.

Iron Man flew over, landing in front of the heavy equipment to assess the situation.

Mallen looked ruthless and savage. He clenched his teeth and crouched, awaiting an attack. The chain swung closer to Tony, faster and faster, as Mallen moved slowly toward Iron Man.

"You really want to do it like this?" Iron Man turned to the backhoe and, in a single motion, ripped the bucket off the tractor. He remembered riding in these when he was little, back when the new Stark Industries office had been under construction. Municipal building records from the original Stark office flashed past Tony's HUD. *I can multitask again,* he thought, grateful for the new speed Extremis had given him.

"I am trying very hard not to kill you," Tony said.

"I only left you alive in Texas because I was busy," Mallen snarled. He swung the chain at Iron Man, who parried with the backhoe bucket. The chain's sling hook caught in the bucket teeth, sparking and breaking.

Iron Man moved to crush Mallen with the bucket. But Mallen dodged easily, then kicked aside the bucket, surprising Tony. Mallen punched Tony with an incredibly powerful left cross. Iron Man felt the impact, and his HUD informed him that a punch had landed, but all he saw was a blur.

Mallen then connected with a backward kick across Iron Man's thigh. Tony aimed a front jab at Mallen's chin, but Mallen caught his fist and started to crush it.

"Ha! Did it again—"

Klang! Tony head-butted Mallen in the teeth so hard that blood sprayed from his nose and mouth.

Mallen fired two massive bolts of electricity at Iron Man, knocking him back.

"RRRRAAAA!" Mallen roared and leapt forward.

Iron Man fell to the ground under Mallen's tackle, cracking the pavement as he touched down.

Tony reeled momentarily, blind rage flashing through his mind. He was suddenly filled with hate, with the desire to kill. He saw himself lying on the pavement, then looked up at the national carousel on the mall. He wanted to smash it, to crush this place where politicians took their children for fun. He wanted to fly to the FBI, to burn it to the ground. And he had some really useless information in his head about skinning rabbits.

What was going on?

Emergent tech, he realized. Extremis hadn't fully taken yet, wasn't entirely bound to him on a molecular level. He'd had it in his system for less than a day, and it was designed to learn from available sources. Iron Man was a work in progress—still evolving, sometimes surprising even himself. And now he had connected to Mallen's internal framework.

Like seeing through satellites, Tony was seeing through Mallen's eyes.

Mallen didn't seem to notice. His veins bulged as he placed his hands around Iron Man's neck and squeezed.

Tony heard the hydraulics in his helmet start to hiss as Mallen cracked open the seal connecting his helmet to his neck guard. *I'm in trouble,* he thought. He felt the pressure of the maniac's fingers pressing in.

And Mallen truly was unhinged. Now that he'd been inside Mallen's head, Tony could see there was no turning back for this lethal killer. This had to end, now.

"Mallen…for God's sake…we both have Extremis in us. Stop this. The future…" said Tony. "Don't make me…"

Mallen screamed at Tony. "If you're the future, I'm going to kill it! I'm murdering the future!"

Tony Stark was choking, his air completely cut off. *One hundred percent,* he thought, glancing at a meter on his HUD and watching his unibeam power level build. Another tweak he'd made to Maya's program. Stark Ocular, his own patent—the one he used in all his Iron Man suits.

Iron Man blasted Mallen with the most powerful unibeam he'd ever shot, blowing a hole directly through Mallen's chest.

Mallen's eyes rolled back in his head, but still he kept his grip on Tony's neck. Tony felt lightheaded and dizzy. *Why isn't he dead yet? How can he still be standing?*

"Gkk!" Tony tried to choke out words. "Mallen, you stupid…"

Mallen lurched left, then right, but somehow he remained standing.

And still tightening his grip on Tony's neck. Mallen was all instinct. Even with blood streaming down his chest, he was still a killer.

There was a way to stop Extremis. One way, the only way.

Tony glanced at his HUD one last time, moving the targeting crosshairs. And fired.

Mallen's head evaporated in a ball of white flame.

His headless body collapsed on to Tony, a hole through the chest. Iron Man gasped for air. Then he struggled to sit up, throwing Mallen's lifeless body to the side with a dull thump.

"Damn you," said Iron Man. "Damn you for making me do that."

He stood up, noticing that his armor was already repairing itself. Extremis was still busy improving him.

"You can't stop the future, Mallen," he said quietly, standing over the dead man. "The future always kills the past."

NINETEEN

Six military police officers in full uniform stood in front of Futurepharm's Austin headquarters. The beige, bland boxiness of the office park looked improved in the darkness, slightly mysterious against the dark-blue night sky. Above, thick swirling clouds gave the evening a deserved air of suspense and drama.

Iron Man's white-and-orange-fired boot jets illuminated his path down as he dropped in front of the building. His internal GPS and night-vision sensors automated his landing. He greeted the MPs as he touched down.

"Let's get this over with," he said.

The men followed him into the lobby. As they approached the front desk, the night security guard stood up.

"Stand down," Iron Man commanded, pointing imperiously at the guard. "We're here on business."

The security guard meekly backed away and sat back down.

Tony led the men up the elevator to Maya's office near Lab 4. It was late, but she was still there. Maya was always at Futurepharm. She'd probably been expecting Tony's arrival. He felt guilty that the visit wasn't social, or a medical follow-up to check on the Extremis process in his body.

She was walking down the hall, carrying some files. She hadn't heard them come in. "Maya," said Iron Man.

She stopped and turned around. When she saw the MPs behind Iron Man, she dropped the files. Her eyes opened wide, and she froze.

"It takes two keys to open the Extremis vault. You told me that," said Iron Man. "Your boss had one. You had one. He couldn't get into the vault to steal the Extremis dose on his own."

She began to shake and back away. She stopped when her back touched the wall. There was nowhere to go.

"I've had time to do some thinking. My team decrypted Killian's records. And my new suit—the one you gave me—wires me into all kinds of networks.

"I know, Maya."

She looked down.

"The Army pulled the Extremis funding," he continued. "No field test, no more money, even though you had a working process. So you and your boss decided to arrange a live demonstration yourselves."

She raised her eyes now, but still looked away.

"Dose a terrorist with Extremis. Then call your old friend Tony Stark, whom you haven't seen in years, but who just happens to also be Iron Man. Show the world a test of your process. The perfect demonstration. An Extremis enhancile pitted against a man wearing the most advanced personal-combat system on earth."

"You know what they said about the atomic bomb," said Maya. She stared straight ahead now, expressionless. "They said it had to be used once in anger, in order that it never be used in anger again."

Two MPs moved to either side of Maya. One of them put a hand firmly on her shoulder. She'd as good as confessed.

"I would have used the renewed funding to get out of the arms race," she continued. "Set up shop on my own. Medical technology. More than fifty people die in car accidents every day. The sacrifice of the Houston FBI was necessary to save lives in the future. Extremis could stop wars. I could cure cancer. I could help all mankind, and only those fifty people had to die. The math made sense."

"Maya, you loosed a super-powered lunatic on the world. Did you think he'd stop after he slaughtered the Houston FBI?"

"You failed, Tony. Iron Man was supposed to beat him the first time."

"Your field test was too good. He wouldn't have stopped with me, Maya. He was going to kill the president, everyone in government. Do you think the military could have stopped him?"

"Someone would have stopped him. Captain America. The Hulk."

"You don't know that. Your behavior was reckless, put thousands of lives at risk. Dr. Killian realized that, and he couldn't live with the knowledge. You still haven't admitted it."

She turned to look at Iron Man now, her eyes furious.

"The only mistake I made was giving a damn about the man inside the Iron Man suit," she said almost in a whisper. "You'd be dead now if Extremis hadn't saved your life, Tony. And it's still evolving. Extremis is unstable—it's too big a responsibility for one man. You're a walking time bomb."

"I can live with that, Maya. You know what I can't live with? Knowing that children lost arms and legs to Stark Enterprises land mines. They wouldn't be impressed that their sacrifices helped me fund heart-medicine research. Those people at the FBI...I don't think their families understand your math. The ends don't justify the means. I know that now. You obviously don't."

"There's no difference between us. You're no better than me, Tony Stark."

Iron Man looked down, quiet and reflective in the lab's shadows. Tony thought about his mission in the world. He raised his head then, and stepped forward into the light.

"But I'm trying to be," he said. "And I'm going to be able to look myself in the mirror tomorrow morning."

"Want a scotch?" Sal Kennedy turned to Tony with a half-smile. He still wore a flower-print shirt and those tinted round glasses, but he looked more tired, less relaxed than he had a few days ago.

"Sal, I told you before. I don't drink anymore."

"Then what are you doing in the local saloon?"

"Looking for you, obviously. Do you think I just stumbled through a bar in Occidental, California, on my way from Texas to Coney Island?"

"Fine, fine, you never just stop by on a social call. You avoid me for years, then you show up twice in one week when you need the kind of unusual thinking only your wise old pal can give." Sal affected a pouting look, then motioned Tony on to the stool next to him. "Again, you need me. Get in line. So does this waitress. She needs my order. You want anything? I get that you don't want a drink, but they have pot pies here. And by pot pies, I mean…"

"I ate on the plane, Sal. You could have saved me the drive to your place and then back to town if you'd buy a phone. You don't even need to buy it. I could get you a real nice one, just like mine. Won't matter if signals don't reach you, works off a satellite I set up myself. I went up into space and everything."

Sal waved him off. "You want to do me a favor, Tony? Work faster. Give me a phone when it's a nanobot I can swallow in a pill. Or make it injectable. Or reverse it: Load me into the phone as part of the coming singularity. No more of this holding things up to my ear. Bad for the shoulder. Anyway, why did you drive? You deliberately *don't* fly to my door just so you'll have something to complain about."

"I don't fly myself to your door so you don't have to explain to the world that you're personal friends with Iron Man. It's okay, though. The drive gave me more time to feel like crap for turning an old friend over to the authorities."

Sal motioned to the newspaper on the bar. "Yeah, I read about that. I wonder if they have yoga class in jail."

Tony looked down and wouldn't meet Sal's eyes.

"Maya doesn't feel any guilt, Sal," he said. "She believes her particular genius is exempt from guilt, and that her funding is worth the lives of several ordinary people. She can't see that Mallen running around passing judgment on who gets to live or die was a problem."

They sat quietly for a moment, side by side. Tony picked up the paper Sal had been reading. *SCIENTIST CHARGED IN HOUSTON FBI INCIDENT.*

"Did you see yesterday's headlines?" Tony asked.

"No, I got in a new shipment of psychedelic Peruvian tea, so I was home yesterday."

"Good," said Tony abruptly.

"Bad behavior is almost impossible to change," said Sal softly. "This isn't your fault. We've been conditioned for thousands of years. The way out—your way out, conscious change—it's almost impossible for most people. Without the use of pharmaceuticals, I mean."

"She'll go to jail, Sal. After she saved my life and upgraded Iron Man."

"She's responsible for the deaths of a lot of people, Tony, and the potential for destruction that she put out into the world…" Sal shook his head.

Tony frowned. Sal was right, but Tony had been given a second chance, third chance, many chances. He'd been irresponsible in his younger days, but Pepper had covered for him until he'd straightened up. He'd been an alcoholic, but managed to quit. He'd lost his company to Stane, then gotten it back. His weapons had killed people, but now that experience was being used to help others.

"Where would I be without second chances?" Tony drummed his fingers on the bar.

"I agree, it's a shame to waste Maya's brilliance on making license plates," said Sal. "What about if we plea-bargain for community service? She can be under my care. I'm teaching in Silicon Valley next spring, a school solely dedicated to futurism. We have a biotech-innovation program she'd be perfect for."

"They won't let her near biotech after this—probably not even near medicine. Maya won't even be able to take a dog's temperature. But I appreciate your offer."

"How about you, then? We have a robotics program, Tony. You could use a change. Why don't you come out and help us teach artificial intelligence?"

"I'll send Jarvis. He mimics how the brain absorbs and learns from information pretty well. He doesn't need me to teach AI. And he'll learn the names of the students faster than I would."

Sal threw back his head and laughed. "AI teaching AI! I'll pitch it. You know, you could have one of your old suits teach the class. People need somewhere to look when they're taught. It'll be like you're there, but you don't even have to leave your boardroom." Tony laughed, too.

Then he leaned forward and frowned. "What do you call it when you produce a weapon that kills people, but you yourself didn't do the killing?"

"Tony…"

"I'm aware of the irony, Sal. Maybe I should be in jail, too. I made weapons. I didn't fire them myself, but they killed a lot of people. I manufactured a weapon—so did Maya. Mine were used to kill people, but I didn't do it myself. Same with Maya. But what I did is legal, even though my weapons killed way more people than Maya's."

"Tony, when you were a little kid, do you remember your mom reading *The Three Little Pigs* to you? Or *Hansel and Gretel*?"

Tony called the waitress over and ordered a seltzer.

"Sal, my mom…I wasn't like that. She read two books to me. One was *Mike Mulligan and His Steam Shovel,* and the other was *The Little Engine that Could.* After that, we switched to *Popular Mechanics* until I was old enough to sit around drawing illustrations to go with Aristotle's *The Physics.* I just wasn't interested in fairy tales."

"You're not helping. You were a weird kid. Look, my point is that when we were younger, good and evil were clear concepts. Three little pigs, good. Big bad wolf, evil. But then you start crossing lines, and things get more complicated from there—*I'll just tell my mother I went straight to bed instead of admitting I was up all night with a flashlight and that new issue of* Popular Mechanics.'"

"What, so reading under the covers at night leads to manufacturing land mines found decades later in Cambodia?"

"Moral ambiguity is the basis for all life's hiccups, Tony. Thing is, you and Maya both crossed lines for all the wrong reasons. You've made munitions that endangered some and protected others. Just being Iron Man puts your staff at risk. How would you feel if your Mrs. Rennie were kidnapped by your enemies?"

"You mean besides worried for the kidnappers?"

Sal smiled. "Seriously, Tony. My point is that there is a difference between you and Maya. She thought her way was the only way. She couldn't change. You have emergent tech in your body, but maybe that's to be expected, because you were already evolving as a human. Now you aren't just working with emergent tech. You *are* emergent tech."

They sat in silence for a moment. The server walked out of the swinging kitchen half-doors, holding a steaming chicken pot pie. She smiled as she placed it on the bar in front of Sal.

Tony started laughing.

"What?" Sal opened his eyes wide with mock exaggeration. "Wait, did you think I meant…?"

"You know what I thought you meant, Sal," said Tony. "Hey, I'm gonna take off. I want to go back to Coney Island. Catch up on some work. Fly around a bit for my fans. Check in with Pepper. She's going to be pissed that I nearly died again. Give me a call next time you're near a pay phone, okay?"

Tony headed out of the bar and stopped next to the entrance. He could see himself in a mirror beneath a coat rack.

"You again," he said, staring at himself for a minute.

He looked back at Sal, who gave him a thumbs up from over his pot pie. Sal waved. Tony grinned. He looked back at the mirror.

"Nice to see you."

TWENTY

"**M**ISTER STARK."

How does Mrs. Rennie do that? Tony wondered again. He'd had a busy week and had neglected to look into how she'd patched the intercom into the surround-sound in his Coney Island garage.

"What now?"

"Do you know who this is, Mister Stark?"

He grinned. He was standing in front of his workbench, working with a life-size holographic schematic of his collapsible armor and a tablet covered with digital data.

"Of course I know. It's Iron Man's biggest fan. The woman who loves Iron Man *so much* that when she was in college, she went to the World's Fair just to meet his father, even though Iron Man and Tony Stark didn't even exist yet."

Mrs. Rennie whistled. "How did you figure that out, Mister Stark?"

"Owen did. Our new intern, the kid you brought on board after his stunt on the Wonder Wheel. I asked him to research a photo I found at the Smithsonian, one showing a college girl batting her eyelashes at Howard Stark, and he decided the girl looked like you. So he showed it to Happy, who—once he stopped snickering—told him to run it past Jarvis for analysis."

"I'll be sure to assign Owen lots of extra photocopying later," said Mrs. Rennie.

"You'll have to wait. He's out right now trying to find a photo lab that can handle 127-format negatives. We located the original and are getting it blown up as a Christmas gift for Mister Rennie. You won't believe the look you were giving my dad. At least, I couldn't believe it. Were you *easy*, Mrs. Rennie?"

"Oh, that's rich, coming from you, Mister Stark. Though I do seem to recall Howard Stark asking for my phone number."

"He did *not*." Tony was horrified. His parents probably hadn't met yet when Mrs. Rennie was in college, but the idea of his crusty old secretary flirting with his father before he was even born was too much for Tony. Suddenly he regretted starting this.

"Whatever you need to imagine to keep yourself happy, Mister Stark. Do you know why I'm calling you?"

"Because Ms. Potts has arrived in the lobby and wants to declare her undying devotion to me?"

"Not likely, Mr. Stark," said Mrs. Rennie. "Try not living in a filthy man cave first. Or not flirting with other women. I hear that helps. No, I'm calling because your company has arrived. Stark's board of directors has assembled in the conference room and is ready for your address. I've tabulated your data, explained the meaning of your statistics, and prepared handouts clarifying my mathematical calculations. I'll have Owen pass them around to the board members."

"Thank you, Mrs. Rennie." There were benefits to hiring a retired algebra teacher. "Can you make sure they have everything they need? Coffee, water…"

"They are all well-supplied with Mango Mermaid products, Mr. Stark. They've been briefed on next-quarter strategy by Ms. Potts and received an update from Markko in Engineering. They've also had lunch, and they are waiting for your address."

"Systems off," said Tony. The holographic display he'd been working with faded and disappeared. He headed out the door, stopping to check out his new business suit in the mirror. Mrs. Rennie really did have good taste in choosing his suits. He stepped outside and headed across the back courtyard to the rear service entrance of Stark Enterprises' Coney Island headquarters.

"I've just uploaded a field-test report of the Stark Beam 01 to each of your tablet computers. I think you'll find it fared exceptionally well on the battlefield, but we'll have to do consumer testing as well, given that most consumers don't have the same needs as Iron Man."

He paused for a laugh. Hearing none and seeing only stony faces from the Stark Enterprises board members assembled around the conference-room table, Tony continued.

"Right. Soooo, Geoff, has any progress been made on assessing potential telecommunications takeover targets?"

Geoff cleared his throat. "Yes, Tony. Acquisitions has found a small, undervalued company that runs on an unpopular band. We have some ideas about how to increase the appeal of this band without giving away our plans until the Stark Beam is out in the marketplace. We'll need to have a strategy discussion with PR. And Markko, who's implementing the upgrade, wants to meet with you on the engineering, since none of us were able to understand his explanation."

"Great. Let's give Markko a bonus. Any objections?" Tony glanced around the room. The board members shook their heads.

"Markko's shrieking space heaters are flying off the shelves," Geoff continued, "and the last-minute upgrade where they can scream in Latin or German was a nice touch. It increased media coverage and, thus, sales."

"Wait," said Tony. "Whose idea was that?"

"Mine," said Geoff, reddening a bit.

"Geoff! Nice touch." Tony chuckled. *Didn't know he had it in him.*

"Thanks. This phone will solve our short-term

money problems, but we're still concerned about future contracts, Tony. All your work with alternative energy hasn't generated results yet."

"Geoff, give it a rest. We weren't even planning to make phones six month ago, and now we're about to corner that market. And if Markko comes up with just a few more smaller ideas as good as his space heater, we'll be just fine while R&D keeps plugging away at alternative energy. Trust me. Where has the stock price gone in the last two weeks?"

"Straight up, Tony," Geoff admitted. "We do trust you. It's just that, sometimes, you get a little caught up in your latest ideas. Then you disappear into your garage or your Iron Man armor, and it's our job to keep the business running smoothly when that happens. So we need to be aware of what you're working on.

"And there's just one more thing."

Ah. Tony had been expecting this. He restrained himself from arguing that the board didn't keep Stark Enterprises running—Pepper did. He needed to stay on topic, since he was about to drop several surprises on the board at once.

So he feigned ignorance and looked at Geoff innocently. "What might that be?"

"We were wondering if you'd given any more thought to stepping down from being CEO, to taking more of a Chief Technologist role. You know, let someone else handle the business end of Stark Enterprises."

"I have. And I've decided to take your advice…"

Tony paused.

"…that I should look to Bill Gates as an example."

The board held its collective breath. Tony slowly looked around the table, catching each member's eyes individually.

"And that is why I've decided to…"

He savored the moment.

"…establish a foundation."

He saw the stares of disbelief. For a minute, he thought Geoff was going to get up and walk out.

"A foundation," said Geoff. He was silent a moment. "To do what?"

"The Stark Acceleration Foundation will support a series of tech incubators, providing mentors, funding, and resources to engineers and startup entrepreneurs in disadvantaged parts of the world. Geoff, what do Afghanistan, Bolivia, and Congo have in common?"

Geoff and the rest of the board looked blankly at Tony. He knew what they were thinking: *What the hell is he talking about?*

"Come on, you guys know this one. Where do we source supplies from?"

Owen, who had brought in the handouts from Mrs. Rennie, piped up from the corner.

"Lithium comes from Bolivia."

"Thank you, Owen. Why does this high-school student know more than my board?"

"Because I read your handout, Mister Stark," Owen admitted, shyly.

"Smart kid," said Tony. "Maybe the rest of you can follow his lead."

The board members scrambled to grab the paper handouts, which Owen had left neatly piled at one end of the table.

"Lithium is used in lightweight batteries for most of our electronic devices," explained Tony. "For now, the world's biggest supplies are located in the salt plains of Bolivia, but huge reserves have also been found in Afghanistan. Most of our high-tech minerals are mined in places that don't have the economic structure for local entrepreneurs or scientists to build their own businesses. Another resource we buy a lot of is coltan. Why? Because it's used in computers and mobile phones, like the Stark Beam 01. Democratic Republic of the Congo has more than half the world's coltan. And what else does DRC have? No, besides *Rumble in the Jungle*. That's right. DRC has a significantly high percentage of the world's war."

Tony paused for a moment. "Can you guys think of anyone who has benefited from war? Someone who maybe owes the victims of war a second chance?

"It's hard to catch a break if you're a kid who loves science and you live in Congo," he continued. "Does anyone else in this room find it ironic that people in countries full of minerals the rest of the world *must have* for its tech can't even start a tech business in their own home countries? When the minerals they need are in their own backyards?" He paused and waited, though he didn't really expect anyone to speak.

"Because I do. I met a man in Dubai whose brother was an Afghani scientist. That scientist had gone to war because there weren't any science jobs for him. And guess what? Now he's dead.

"When I announced we were abandoning weapons contracts, that was a start. When I put on the Iron Man armor to fight for peace, I started seeing my plan more clearly. But I need—*we* need—to do more. This is an opportunity to help people help themselves, to create something sustainable. We need to get opportunity out there to innovators who have a clear understanding of basic human needs. Why? Because we can help them, sure...but also, they can help us.

"There *is* profit in helping people. Maybe not today, maybe not in a year. But if we can help people develop their own resources, we will ultimately find a way to benefit from these alliances."

"Tony..." Geoff was, as usual, the voice of caution. "We can't send businesspeople out into the Congolese bush as mentors. There aren't suitable lodgings or medical facilities. Where are we going to mentor these entrepreneurs? There aren't even research labs."

"Give me a *little* credit, Geoff." Tony rolled his eyes. "What do you think Pepper's been doing on her overseas mission? She's got it all worked out for Congo, because that's where we're going first—and, of course, because she's smart. We've salvaged an old German steamship, which is being refitted now with modern tech, labs, classrooms, cafes, and cabins. It's going to be dismantled in Dar es Salaam, then shipped by train to Lake Tanganyika, where we'll put it back together and sail over to DRC from there. Staff will all come in via Zambia or Tanzania."

The board didn't seem too enthused. Tony knew what the next question was before Geoff opened his mouth.

"How do you propose to pay for this endeavor?" Refitting German steamships with the most modern technology in the world doesn't come cheap, Tony knew.

"I'm glad you asked that, Geoff. Owen, can you pass around the next handout? Thanks." Owen distributed the paper showing Mrs. Rennie's calculations.

"Tony, I see huge profits here that are meant to directly fund this 'resource incubator,' as you term it in the handout. But I don't understand where the profits are coming from. The phone and appliance divisions' proceeds are intended to fund the company, not your charity project."

"It's not charity, Geoff. In time, there will be profit from this, but indirectly. Think of it like this: Let's say China or the U.S. builds a road in a country with vast mineral resources. Then, whoa, a few years later they get all kinds of great advantages when they ask if they can mine in that country. Would you call that road charity? Or would you call it foresight? Or just plain smart? Our business incubator takes that strategy a step further. We get an actual percentage of ownership of companies we help start in exchange for our support."

"Regardless, there will be a gap during which time we have no funding for this, uh…foundation."

"Jarvis, project Iron Man licensing," muttered Tony. The holographic projector above the conference-room table lit up, and holograms of Iron Man T-shirts, stickers, lunch boxes, and video games suddenly filled the room. Owen gasped and smiled. The board members hesitated, then pushed forward for a closer look.

"Another side project Pepper's been working on. Iron Man licensing. Instant money, fully funding the new foundation, with enough left over to build another Zipsat satellite."

"I have to admit, Tony, this is impressive."

"Of course it is, Geoff. Oh, and look at this." Tony held up a thick paper document. "I've agreed to demonstrate Iron Man—the new version, Extremis—for *Billionaire Boys and their Toys.* Not only do I get paid for the appearance, and that money goes straight to the foundation, but also—free advertising for our Iron Man T-shirts. Nice, huh? That wasn't my idea, by the way. That was Pepper's. Well, sort of. At least, she said if I liked the show so much, why didn't I just go on it already and shut up about it."

"Well, Tony," said Geoff. "You've outdone yourself here. You really do seem dedicated to saving the world, and the board is behind you on that a hundred percent. But I'm looking at this handout you gave us here, and you wrote out a statement of purpose for Stark Enterprises across the top."

"You mean the part about how our goal is to bring on the future and be a part of it? That's really what we're all about, Geoff. You're not planning to argue with me about that, are you? Because if you are—"

Geoff interrupted him. "No, no. The board agrees

with that statement. And that is why I'm proposing a change to your foundation."

Tony looked apprehensively at Geoff. *Uh-oh.*

"Let's change the name. Let's call it something snazzy. Like this line you typed here."

"Where?"

"Here." He pointed to his copy of the handout. "*Test Pilots for the 21st Century.*"

Tony felt tears welling up, so he said nothing. He just stood up and applauded Geoff. And then the rest of the board members rose, too. Not only to applaud Geoff, but to applaud Tony, Owen, Iron Man licensing, and the direction in which the company was going.

Stark Enterprises was heading into the future.

EPILOGUE

Maya awoke to the sound of a rooster crowing incessantly.

"It's still dark, you stupid bird," she muttered. A seven-year-old Congolese child in a tattered Obama 2008 T-shirt lay snuggled up next to her. He fluttered his eyes open, and she regretted speaking her thoughts aloud.

"Go back to sleep, kid," she whispered. But already, the twelve other people sleeping in the canvas-covered bed of the old Mercedes truck were stirring and stretching. None of them had slept all that well on the sacks of flour, onions, and live goats that served as a communal mattress. There was no way they could ignore the rooster-snooze-alarm.

She heard the cab doors open, then both the driver and truck mechanic rolled out and landed in the mud bog under the truck.

"Bonjour," said the driver. He was cheerful even though he'd spent the night in a bog after driving for fourteen hours yesterday. "Let's dig out the bus and get going," he added in French.

A few of the passengers climbed out, and one middle-aged Zambian man in acid-washed jeans with fake gem studs on them handed out shovels and pickaxes from the back of the truck. Six men tackled the muddy bog in the first light of the morning sun. They'd alternately dig out mud, then stop long enough to find rocks, which they'd throw under the tires, rebuilding the road as they went.

The steady slap and thud of tools digging in the mud was rhythmic, and Maya dozed off for another hour. Eventually, she heard the truck start up.

"D'accord," yelled one man. "Go ahead." He signaled thumbs up to the driver, and everyone on the ground stood back.

The driver revved the engines, then slowly put the truck into gear. It lurched forward. He switched gears furiously, one foot pressed down hard on the accelerator, the other foot stabbing at the clutch. The truck slid back, and he gave it gas again. Back and forth, back and forth the driver rocked the Mercedes. Maya would have been alarmed, except that something like this happened every time she went to a village to assess a tech entrepreneur's potential market.

The tires burned black smoke. The driver cut the engine.

The passengers sighed. A grandmother in eyeglasses and an orange-and-brown wax-print dress and head wrap put her feet up on a sack of onions. The men who had been digging the truck free went back to work, digging out more mud and dropping more rocks in under the tires. Maya noticed the tire had barely any tread left. How old was this truck?

The rooster was still crowing, and the goats in the back of the truck were bleating now, desperate to get free of the ropes around their ankles.

"I know the feeling," said Maya. She wore an electronic-surveillance ankle bracelet that was impossible for her to remove on her own

Just then she heard the sounds of greetings.

"*Bonjour!*" Two men, clean of mud, had approached, walking from down the road.

"We have come here to find you," said the older man in the clean, pressed suit jacket. "We were waiting in town, and the bus—it is very late."

"Let's go find the bus, said my father," added his son, a younger man in jeans and a Green Bay Packers T-shirt.

"Town is close by?" Maya interrupted them.

"Of course, *madam*," said the son. "If you had all just walked two kilometers, you could have had dinner, then stayed the night in beds, under mosquito nets, in the guesthouse. We watched a football game in town last night. An enjoyable evening."

The passengers sighed. The grandmother shook her head and smiled. She'd been facing life's little disappointments for sixty-five years.

"May I walk back with you?" Maya asked.

"Mais oui."

Maya handed the kid in the Obama shirt to his mother. She took off her flip-flops, then slid down out of the truck bed, landing barefoot with a squish in some reddish mud.

"Oh, ick," she exclaimed involuntarily. The son extended an arm to Maya, and she handed him her knapsack and flip-flops. She waded out of the bog.

The Congolese giggled at Maya's horrified expression as she stared at her mud-caked feet. Then the father gallantly took her by the elbow and walked her to a large puddle. He pointed to the rainwater, then to her feet. Yes, that seemed like a good plan.

Maya rinsed the mud out from between her toes, then reached out to the son for her flip-flops. She eased herself out of the puddle and gently tip-toed to dry off on the grass.

"Shall we go?" The other passengers waved cheerily. They'd see Maya a few hours, or maybe a day, later. Whenever the sun and shovels cooperated to get the truck moving again.

She followed the father and son, moving from the grass to the potholed dirt road as her flip-flops dried. They walked single file, using the ridges between potholes almost as balance beams between the puddles. The mud bogs that were so dangerous to a truck were easily skirted on foot.

"C'est bon, madam?" The father occasionally turned to check on Maya. She smiled and nodded. Yes, she'd spent the night curled up with goats and children, but there was something impossibly optimistic about the rising sun on an African morning. Here were people who owned very little—maybe some goats, chickens, and a mobile phone—but they were kinder to her than anyone had been at home. She thought she understood why now. At home, she'd allowed the stress from her job to carry over into how she dealt with people. She'd been angry when driving, rude to supermarket cashiers, and furious with colleagues. No wonder she'd been miserable. And people had been miserable to her in return.

Maya took a deep breath and inhaled fresh, clean air that seemed to float over directly from thick rainforest a half a country away. Then she caught a bit of her own insecticide with her morning air, and choked for a second. The son glanced at her quickly, saw that she was fine, and continued walking.

Maya heard more than just their footsteps now. She heard chickens pecking at their morning feed and the distant sound of children playing. The father and son led her through fields to the center of town, a dirt strip surrounded by about ten large, brick buildings and a dozen smaller buildings made of mud and wood.

There was no traffic in town aside from motorbikes, chickens, and bicycles. The father and son led Maya straight to the town guesthouse, a rugged, brick building that acted also as café, bar, television venue, and mobile-phone refill center. Aside from a small church on the other end of town, this was the center of village life.

"Do you have a shower here?" Maya felt gross. She'd slept covered in DEET to avoid getting bitten by mosquitoes in the open air.

"*Oui,*" said the shopkeeper, a tall, bald entrepreneur dressed all in white, which was remarkable given the dust in the countryside. He fetched a bucket and towel, then motioned to her to follow. Behind the restaurant was a cinderblock building covered in a corrugated sheet-metal roof, divided into two small compartments. He stopped to fill the bucket at a spigot, then carried it into one of the compartments. He motioned her in, holding open the ramshackle door for her.

"*Merci,*" said Maya, taking the towel. She stripped off her dirty clothes and hung them high on a nail hammered into the side of the doorframe. She splashed herself with the water using a plastic mug she found floating in the bucket. She doused her electronic ankle bracelet, but that didn't matter. Damn thing was waterproof. Probably nuclear-war proof, she figured.

I need to remember to carry soap on these expeditions, Maya thought. She'd had to remember a lot of things on her forays into the Congolese countryside. The contrast between her high-tech cabin back on the ship in Lake Tanganyika and the situation here was stark, though the locals didn't seem to mind anywhere near as much as she did.

She'd carried peanut butter, bug spray, bread, plastic utensils, a sheet, treated water, a fork, duct tape, antibacterial gel, toilet paper, and a utility knife along, but these day-long expeditions never lasted only a day. The condition of the roads and "bus," as the locals called the truck, were such that breakdowns weren't just common, they were a given. She was torn between being more prepared or just going local. The Congo residents were stoic, sleeping in the clothes on their backs, seemingly unworried by their lack of packable duct tape.

Still, working on Stark Enterprises' tech incubator on site in Congo was preferable to the four months she'd spent in prison back in Texas. She'd only seen the sun once a week, for twenty minutes at a stretch, had only water and milk to drink, and hadn't been fond of the high-fat diet or the once-weekly towel exchange. She'd been able to buy candy or chips from the commissary, but the occasional cheap chocolate bar hadn't exactly made the situation tolerable. She'd been allowed to choose books off the donated books cart, but there was barely anything worth reading. Awful books, bestsellers and romances. Books about implausible science experiments gone wrong, where the author just threw in some tech terms to dazzle the reader. Maya was an avowed atheist, but she'd even read the Bible out of desperation.

She was glad now to have studied the Bible in prison. So many of the people she met in the countryside were devoutly religious.

And then Maya heard a distant roar of engines over her splashing. The truck had made it out of the bog. But also, there was a second sound. A familiar sound. One she knew all too well.

Boot jets, she thought.

"Madam Maya," Maya heard a small child calling to her from outside the shower.

"Un monstre! The monster wishes to see you, please come!"

Outside of the FBI, only one person could find her no matter where she went. Only her supervisor had access to the Zipsat tracking signal emitted by her ankle bracelet.

"Tell Iron Man to wait. I'm not hurrying for him."

Tony Stark. Maya tried to work up the hatred she'd felt for him during those months in prison, but found she could not. She tried then to remember the passion she'd had for him in the early days—years ago, when she'd seen only his brilliance. Before she realized how frail Tony's ego was, how damaged he was from growing up with an inattentive, wealthy, alcoholic genius for a father. Before she saw him use the attention of women to make himself feel more appealing and desirable.

Maya could find neither hate nor love within her soul. To her surprise, she felt only compassion for the people she was helping. Back at Futurepharm, she'd been singularly devoted to her job, had never socialized, and had few friends. Here, people accepted her easily, made her laugh, and gave names and faces to the bigger world she'd always imagined herself to be helping. When she thought of the man she'd injected with the last remaining Extremis dose, she was surprised at her own ambivalence. She'd never expected to put Tony Stark's betrayal behind her so quickly.

She remembered her fury at Tony. Here was a man

who had failed to stop Mallen outside Houston, whose failure had killed several people in fiery car crashes. A man who was never punished for his failures, while she had been sent to prison and forbidden access to all medical technology, to all the tools of her field. Tony was allowed to walk freely in spite of creating weapons that still haunted former fields of war, while she had been punished simply for running a research trial.

Stark was no longer a weapons designer. Now he was a walking weapon. Or had the potential to be. What would happen if he ever lost control? If he started drinking again? Long-term, Maya's serum hadn't been tested. What if it reshaped Iron Man again, in ways he didn't anticipate?

But that was the future. Right now Tony was out flying around the world enjoying himself, while Maya was stuck in Congo, restricted to a 100-mile radius. Sometimes she fantasized that the bracelet on her leg would shut off so she could disappear into the forest. She'd head west by truck to Kinshasa, then across the river to start the long journey north through Gabon, Nigeria and Senegal—all the way to Morocco, then by ferry to Spain. What she wouldn't give for some *tapas* right now, and a day on the beach of the Mediterranean.

She finished cleaning herself up as best she could, dried off, and put her dirty clothes back on. Maya dumped the bucket of gray water out on a small vegetable garden behind the brick shower shed and headed back up front to the cafe, her hair still sopping wet. She was quickly covered in sweat again from the heat of the day—she'd need another shower later.

Maya could see Iron Man up at the town's dirt road, where the arriving truck had parked without bothering to move to one side or the other. There was no other traffic here.

Iron Man hovered against the sky, his boot jets firing dramatically as he sparkled red and gold against the bright-blue morning. He held the front of the truck aloft while the truck mechanic lay underneath, cleaning up after the journey over rocks and mud.

"Un moment," yelled the mechanic from under the Mercedes.

"Pas de probleme," said Tony. "Hey, Maya."

She hadn't realized Tony had seen her—but of course, he didn't have to. Her ankle bracelet would have registered on his HUD.

The mechanic crawled away from the truck and stood up, giving Iron Man a thumbs up. Iron Man lowered the Mercedes gently, without so much as a bounce.

Iron Man's hydraulics hissed ever so slightly as his engines cut, and he landed with a faint clank. Maya noticed with some satisfaction that he'd gotten mud on his shiny armor.

A small child cowered, fled to Maya, and hid his head in her armpit.

"C'est bon," kid. It's okay." Maya patted the little boy on the back.

Iron Man walked over to the café now. He didn't clank as much as he used to, Maya noticed. The more intimate control Tony had over the suit now made it more a part of him, less a prosthesis.

Tony looked at the plastic chair where Maya was sitting and shook his head. "Suit off," he said. The joints inside the suit disengaged, parts of the armor retracting and others simply hovering. "Fold," said Tony. The suit folded itself up into a small, neat package, which lowered itself on to the ground.

"Nice trick," said Maya, icily. "But you're scaring the children."

"Nah, kids love me. You should have seen them back at the mud bog when I pulled the truck out. I had to stop them from climbing on top of me while I was working."

"Hey, Iron Man." The truck driver—who was jolly, bald, and round in his tank top with his belly hanging out—walked up and fist-bumped Tony. "Nice job you did back there. I didn't really want to spend another night in a bog. At least not until tomorrow. Can I buy you a beer?"

"No, thanks," said Tony. But he waved the shop-keeper over and asked for a sugary soft drink. Now that he'd taken off his climate-controlled suit, his skin was starting to shine with sweat like everyone else's.

"So, Maya. I'm here for a progress report on the Congo program. How are our entrepreneurs coming along?"

"Why didn't you just use Zipsat to radio the ship like Mrs. Rennie does?"

Tony muttered something that Maya couldn't hear.

"What?"

"I said, it's a condition of your parole that I see you in person once a month."

Maya sat down to pull out her bread, utility knife, and chunky peanut butter. As she spread peanut butter on the first slice of bread, two scrawny children ran to her elbows.

"*S'il vous plaît, madam.*" They looked at her with big, sad eyes.

Maya cracked a smile now. These urchins knew a softie when they saw one. And that's what she was now. Humbly helping others with no potential for self-aggrandizement or personal reward. The only person getting credit for the Stark tech incubator was the man who had paid for it: Tony Stark.

She handed over the bread slices. The kids tried to be polite and formal—children were so well-mannered here—but they were too excited to maintain that charade. They nearly shrieked with excitement.

"Where'd you get the peanut butter?" Tony asked. "There's no supermarket on the ship."

"One of our entrepreneurs is creating mini 3D helicopters—they're not much bigger than your arm. They transport lightweight items by flying above roads—you might've noticed the roads here aren't the best. But these copters can detect the road and follow it, so long as you don't give them too many choices to make. They run on peanut oil—peanuts are local—so we have loads of peanuts hanging around. I had one of the interns look up how to make peanut butter. Why not? Another use for something the entrepreneur was already growing. We added a vitamin mixture to the peanut butter. Supercharges their nutrition, and the kids don't know the difference."

"Sounds useful," said Tony. "Like FedEx for remote villages. Plus bonus peanut butter. Has he worked out a plausible price point for mini-helicopter deliveries?"

Maya shook her head. "Our sales mentor is trying to help him sort it out. That's where we always run into problems. We end up having to use phone time as currency. But no one has enough money to buy phone time, so we charge almost nothing, and then the entrepreneurs can't sustain their businesses. Give it time. The economy here is in its infancy."

"How are the other entrepreneurs doing? And the staff?"

Maya was glowing with pride. She nearly forgot that she was speaking to her jailer.

"Brilliant. We've got people working with power inverters and solar energy, gorilla-conservation games for mobile-phone platforms, and a fantastic bartering app that works by text message. We don't even need money for that, if we can sell it to be bundled by the telecom companies."

Maya suddenly recognized she was being too enthusiastic—that was no way to keep Tony Stark feeling bad for what he'd done to her. She scowled and tried to look angry, but one of the kids squeaked with fear, and she burst out laughing instead.

"Maya," Tony said slowly. "I appreciate the work you're doing."

"Well, it is an improvement over sitting in a tiny cell with three other women while reading the Bible all day. But I'm still pissed at you, Tony. If I hadn't rebuilt your body, you would have died."

"And the thanks you get is you're outside, out in the world, learning empathy and helping people who need your help, in sustainable ways that can make a genuine difference. And you don't have to beat anyone up to do it. I envy you, Maya. This is a dream job."

She nodded her agreement now.

"But there's one thing," said Tony. "When you said you're formulating the peanut butter to supercharge the nutrition of local children…look, I'm not saying that's a bad thing. It isn't. But you're treading dangerously close to fields you're forbidden from working in. That's violating the terms of your parole."

"Roger that, boss," said Maya. "I don't touch it myself. The intern did the research. The kitchen puts it together. I just carry it around in my bag in case I get hungry."

Tony nodded and decided to let it go.

"All right, Maya, I'm taking off. Nice work you're doing here. You have six more months, then we move to the next incubator in Bolivia. The ship can't go there, though. We might try building a facility out of salt. Look it up. Oh, wait, I forgot—you're not allowed Internet access." Tony winced. "You'll see it when you get there."

"I'd like to send two of our students to Sal's weird tech school in Silicon Valley, if he'll give them free tuition. Can you ask someone to look into visa issues?"

"Sure. Tell Mrs. Rennie on her next radio call. I'll mention to her I approved it."

Tony stood up and held his arms out while his armor snapped back on. He walked back out to the dirt road next to the Mercedes, and fired up his boot jets. A group of kids ran out to the truck to watch Iron Man streak away into the sky.

Maya stayed where she was for a minute, feeding peanut butter to kids.

"Are you ready, madam?" She turned around to see the shopkeeper waiting for her. He was also the local medic. "We've assembled the medications you sent out by mini-helicopter, and your patients are waiting. We have a teenager showing acute respiratory inflammation from malaria, a pregnant woman with HIV, and a grandmother displaying symptoms of a bacterial intestinal infection. We waited until you were alone, as you requested."

Maya took the medical supplies and followed the shopkeeper into the back of the shop, where her patients lay waiting. Her ankle bracelet would reflect a change of only forty feet. She'd walked farther when she used the bathhouse.

She was violating her parole, but helping these people overcome illnesses was her second chance. It was worth the risk. They had no doctor, and the nearest clinic was days away on these terrible roads.

Perhaps, by caring for these rural Congolese, she could, in some small way, make up for the deaths of the people Mallen had killed.

To not be allowed to help them, to watch them die, would be a fate worse than any punishment Tony Stark or the justice system could dish out.

Besides, she thought, *if I let them die, I'd never be able to look at myself in the mirror again.*

THE END

ACKNOWLEDGMENTS

Writing a book is challenging—and occasionally relentless—under any circumstances, but me writing an entire novel was made possible by the encouragement of three old friends.

One was editor Stuart Moore, who nudged me along, constantly reminding me that life would eventually return to what passes for normal in my odd world. Another was author Warren Ellis, who wrote the comic book series this book is based on. He offered me complete certainty that I could pull this off when I wasn't so sure. Last, the artist-turned-writer-turned-artist Steve Pugh never stopped offering support. He'd taken Alice Hotwire, a character originally created by Warren, and made her his own.

Could it be done? With a little help, yes. I am lucky enough to know the sorts of people who can answer the question, "How does Iron Man go into space" without a moment of hesitation. "Space armor, duh. Where have you been?"

Other ideas and encouragement came from Marc Siry, Steve Buccellato, David Wohl, Shannon Wheeler, Howard Mackie, Michael Kraiger, Carl Potts, Roberta Melzl, Ed Ward, Denise Rodgers, Monica Kubina, and my mom. The hive mind of social networking was always helpful (and often hilarious), such as when Jack Tavares helped name the space plane.

Thank you to Warren and Adi Granov for reimagining Iron Man for the modern world, and giving me complex material and the occasional surprise to work from. Even on the third or fourth reading, I put together things I'd missed before. And thanks to Spring Hoteling for her ever prompt, clean designs, Axel Alonso and Stuart for letting me do this, and Jeff Youngquist for being one of the most remarkably efficient editors I've ever come across.

And last, thanks to those people who unexpectedly seeped in here: My sister, childhood neighbors and people I worked with in fast food in Alexandria, Virginia, Frankie taking me to the camel races in Kuwait, and the random stranger I met in Congo. "We don't need aid or roads," he said. "We are educated people, just like you. What we need is jobs."

That's where I got the idea for Tony Stark's tech incubator.

I just wish it were real.